Patte Gimlin

Bigfoot Film 1967
By Leroy Blevins Sr.

Leroy Blevins Sr.
©2016

Chapters

Ch:1: My Story / Research on Bigfoot.   Pg. 7

Ch:2: The Story   Pg. 53

Ch:3: Roger Patterson's Book   Pg. 81

Ch:4: Documentary   Pg. 89

Ch:5: Copyrights   Pg. 103

Ch:6: Filming Location   Pg. 108

Ch:7: Bigfoot Suit   Pg. 117

Ch:8: My copy of the Suit   Pg. 143

Ch:9: Editing   Pg. 172

Ch:10: Analyzing the Film   Pg. 186

Ch:11: When was the Film Shot?   Pg. 217

Ch:12: Who Wore the Suit?   Pg. 243

Ch:13: Walking Test   Pg. 252

Ch:14: Who Filmed Roger Patterson?   Pg. 267

Ch:15: Notes   Pg. 276

Note from the Author

This book is not out to prove or disprove the existence of a Sasquatch/Bigfoot. This book is based on research and evidence I have uncovered in the last eleven years of intensive investigation into the Patterson and Gimlin (P/G) Bigfoot film and other films that surround it.

In the nearly 50 years since the PG Bigfoot film was shot, scientists and independent researchers have studied the film to prove the creature captured on the film was a real uncatalogued animal. However, when they completed their reports on this film, all they had produced were more questions than answers.

Here is an example: How can anyone claim the creature captured on the film is real? No one who ever studied the film observed a Bigfoot, let alone discovered the body of one of the creatures, and certainly not in 1967 when the film was shot.

It only takes one question to surface, and then after that, another question will arise. There is no easy answer. Soon you have more questions than answers.

This is why the film is still hotly debated today.

I would like to say that when I performed my investigation into the P/G film, I kept my mind open and looked at the available facts from all sides.

I do believe in the existence of Sasquatch/Bigfoot. I saw one myself in 2002. Seeing one myself helped me in my research. When studying the film, I knew what to look for.

Before we get started with our investigation of this film, I want to talk about my encounter. Then I will present my research on the _real_ Sasquatch/Bigfoot. You will see first-hand that this research is not about a new story, but a search for the truth.

Thank you and God Bless.

Chapter One: My Story / Research on Bigfoot

Bigfoot, Yeti, Sasquatch, Wild Man, Skunk Ape, Abominable Snowman, and Neanderthal.

These are just some names of this one type of creature that lives in forests all over the world, including in the United States. Nevertheless, the question is: Does this type of creature exist today or did **it** ever exist?

Even though researchers have been looking for evidence to prove this type of creature does exist today, some people are still skeptical. People have been reporting sightings for the last several thousands of years. In my quest for the truth, I have spent thirteen years going over reports and Bigfoot sightings dating back to ancient times.

I myself do believe in this type of creature. I **saw** one face to face in 2002.

Here is my story.

Date: August 14, 2002

Day: Wednesday

Time: 4:01 p.m.

As I and my crew were driving home from work, we were heading **down** Highway 275 through Kentucky. I was filling out a work report. One of my workers yelled out, "Look, is that a monkey?" I looked up and said, "That is no monkey!" I asked the driver to pull over.

I got out of the truck and walked over by the fence line that was situated about sixty-five feet from the highway. There were a lot of woods along the fence line. As I got closer, the "thing" stood up all the way. I got to within about 20 to 25 feet from it before I stopped. The creature was looking right back at me. You can see all the details of this man in an accompanying drawing.

I use the word "man" because from what I saw, the creature had masculine features, was around 7'4," and had hair covering his body and his face. The body and face was that of a human man, not an ape. After a few minutes, he turned around, stepped over the four-foot fence that was behind him and walked away off into the woods. I walked back to the truck and asked my crew how long I had stood there. They said it was about ten minutes. They looked at me intently and asked me what I had seen. All I could tell them was that I had observed a man with hair that covered his body and that he was around 7'4" tall.

When I returned home that day, I started to do research on what I had seen. This sighting launched my interest in researching Bigfoot.

Drawing I made after I saw the creature.

My investigation focused on what type of man I had seen and where and when did this breed of man begin.

When talking about Bigfoot, researchers refer to them as a "creature." After my sighting, I knew this was no dumb creature of the woods. It was a man like me, but the only difference between me and him was the fur that covered his body. The hair was reddish brown coarser thicker than a normal man's hair, and the size of this man was much larger than normal.

After repeatedly reviewing my sighting, I remembered a story told in the Bible about a man named Esau who had fur covering his body. I studied the story, and from the evidence I uncovered, Esau marked the time when the human race began.

Before we go over the story of Esau, we have to look at the fact that the marking of time in ancient days was a lot different than today, specifically when we note the date that events occur. It all depends on what time period we are studying, such as the time of the beginning of the earth, or the time Esau lived. When researchers study the events described in the Bible or even non-Biblical subjects, they look at time lines.

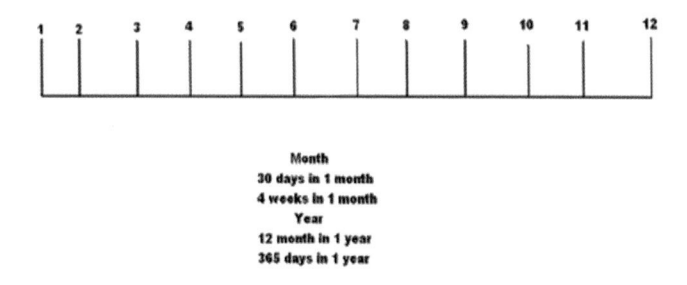

Month
30 days in 1 month
4 weeks in 1 month
Year
12 month in 1 year
365 days in 1 year

This is the conventional time line often referred to when cotemporary researchers put dates on the subjects they are studying. Researchers look at 4 weeks in 1 month, 30 days in 1 month, 12 months in 1 year, 365 days in 1 year. This is the accepted time line used today, and when we perform research on a subject within the time frame of 2,716 years, we use this time line. However, if we try to date any subject before the time frame of 2,716 years, we have to look at how the ancient time frame was described.

For example, from the beginning of time and all the way up to 700 BC, there were no January or February months in Western man's calendar year.

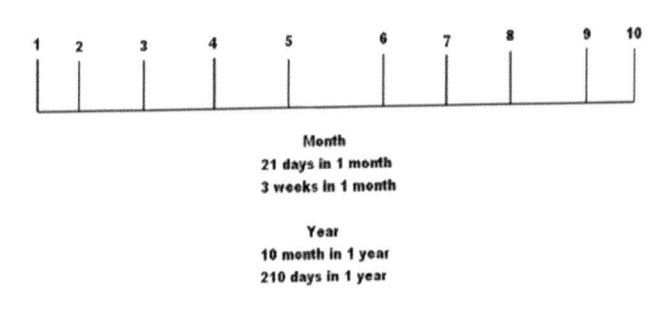

Month
21 days in 1 month
3 weeks in 1 month

Year
10 month in 1 year
210 days in 1 year

In the beginning all the way up to 700 BC, there were only 3 weeks in 1 month, 21 days in 1 month, 10 months in 1 year, and 210 days in 1 year. Using this structuring of time, we can now place true dates on any known subject from the ancient past.

I point out this fact to demonstrate that more exacting dates can be placed on events from the far distant past.

11

Researchers can now place true dates and time lines on their subject matter of interest.

Now on to my research on the first Sasquatch/Bigfoot, which I determine to be Esau.

The story of Esau is found in the first book of the Bible, "Genesis."

Genesis, Chapter 25

V 20: And Isaac was forty years old when he took Rebekah to wife, the daughter of Bethuel the Syrian of Padanaram, the sister to Laban the Syrian.

V21: And Isaac entreated the Lord for his wife, because she was barren: and the Lord was entreated of him, and Rebekah his wife conceived.

V22: And the children struggled together within her: and she said, If it be so, why am I thus? And she went to inquire of the Lord.

V23: And the Lord said unto her, Two nations are in thy womb, and two manner of people shall be separated from thy bowels; and the one people shall be stronger than the other people; and the elder shall serve the younger.

V24: And when her days to be delivered were fulfilled, behold, there were twins in her womb.

V25: And the first came out red, all over like a hairy garment; and they called his name Esau.

V26: And after that came his brother out, and his hand took hold on Esau's heel; and his name was called Jacob: and Isaac was threescore years old when she bare them.

V27: And the boys grew: and Esau was a cunning hunter, a man of the field; and Jacob was a plain man, dwelling in tents.

Break

As stated in V27, Esau was a hunter and lived in the **fields; his** brother Jacob was a plain man that lived in tents.

Esau and Jacob were twins. However, there were some differences between the two brothers. Esau was a man with hair covering his body, and he was a hunter living in the fields. As for Jacob, he was a plain man like all the rest of his people and lived as they did in tents. We continue.

V28: And Isaac loved Esau, because he did eat of his venison: but Rebekah loved Jacob.

V29: And Jacob sod pottage: and Esau came from the field, and he was faint:

V30: And Esau said to Jacob, Feed me, I pray thee, with that same red pottage; for I am faint: therefore, was his name called E-dom.

Break

In summary, Esau was a cunning hunter, and he hunted and killed animals for food for his father. However, when Esau was faint of hunger he did not go out to kill for food but asked his brother Jacob for the food that he was making, which was red pottage (lentil soup).

V31: And Jacob said, Sell me this day thy birthright.

V32: And Esau said, Behold, I am at the point to die: and what profit shall this birthright do to me?

V33: And Jacob said, Swear to me this day; and he swear unto him: and he sold his birthright unto Jacob.

V34: Then Jacob gave Esau bread and pottage of lentils; and he did eat and drink, and rose up, and went his way: thus Esau despised his birthright.

Break

In the first part of the story of Esau, Esau was the first-born son of Isaac; but he sold his birthright to his brother for some red pottage for he was about to die of hunger. As a hunter, Esau only hunted and killed food for his father and not for himself. Thus, Esau was a man that did not eat meat—he was a vegetarian.

Esau's name was changed to Edom for selling his birthright to his brother. As it was done in the old days, the first-born son gets the blessing from his father, and he receives everything his father owns. The younger son serves the oldest brother.

Studying Esau in the first part of the story reveals what Esau looked like, what he ate, and how he lived.

Red lentil

Red lentil is a bean that grown in the ground and when cooked it turns into a paste-like dip. This is what Jacob was cooking and fed Esau for his birthright.

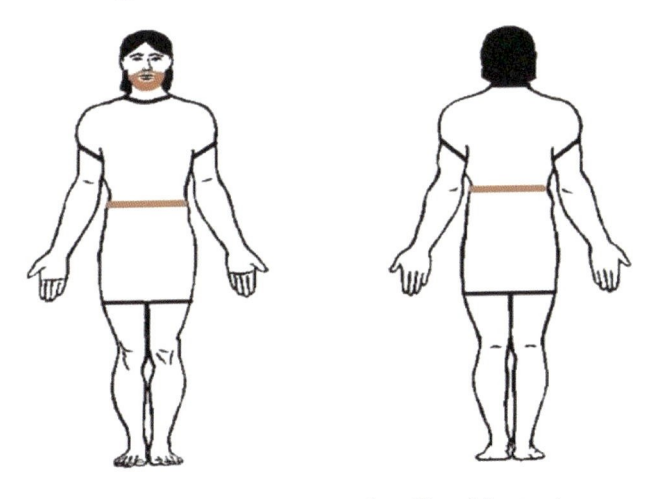

Jacob was a plain man that lived in tents.

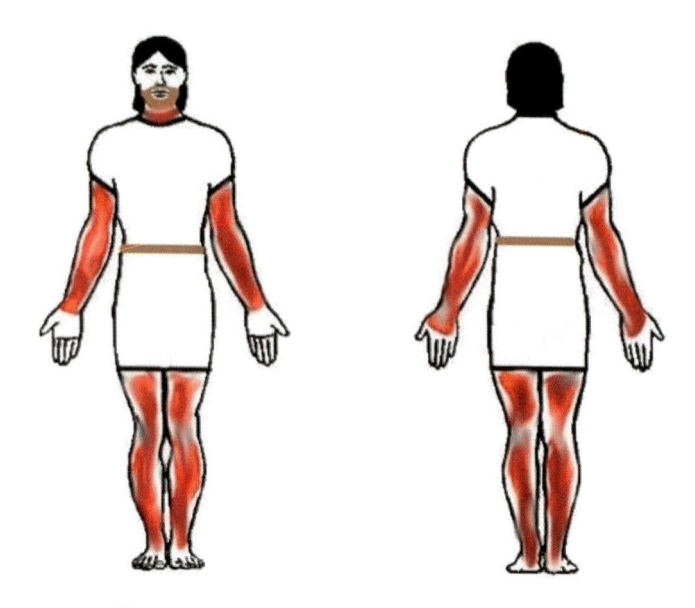

Esau was a man that lived in the fields.

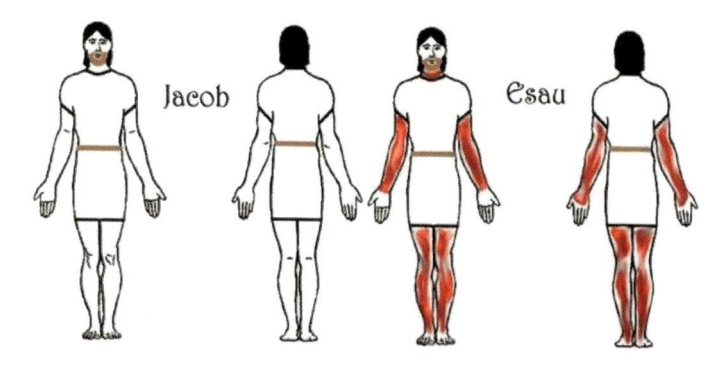

Jacob   Esau

Esau and Jacob were twins. As twins, their features were the same, and they were the same size. However, the difference between both men is that Esau had red hair

16

covering his whole body and Jacob did not have hair all over his body.

The first part of the story of Esau is in chapter 25 - V:20 through V:34 of Genesis. The story continues in Chapter 27.

Genesis Chapter 27

V1: And it came to pass, that when Isaac was old, and his eyes were dim, so that he could not see, he called Esau his eldest son, and said unto him, My son: and he said unto him, Behold, here am I.

V2: And he said, Behold now, I am old, I know not the day on my death:

V3: Now therefore take, I pray thee, thy weapons, thy quiver and they bow, and go out to the field, and take me some venison;

V4: And make me savory meat, such as I love, and bring it to me, that I may eat; that my soul may bless thee before I die.

V5: And Rebekah heard when Isaac speak to Esau his son. And Esau went to the field to hunt for venison, and to bring it.

V6: And Rebekah speak unto Jacob her son, saying, Behold, I heard they father speak unto Esau they brother, saying,

V7: Bring me venison, and make me savory meat, that I may eat, and bless thee before the Lord before my death.

V8: Now therefore, my son, obey my voice according to that which I command thee.

V9: Go now to the flock, and fetch me from thence two good kids of the goats; and I will make them savory meat for thy father, such as he loveth:

V10: And thou shalt bring it to thy father, that he may eat, and that he may bless thee before his death.

V11: And Jacob said to Rebekah his mother, Behold, Esau my brother is a hairy man, and I am a smooth man:

V12: My father peradventure will feel me, and I shall seem to him as a deceiver; and I shall bring a curse upon me, and not a blessing.

Break

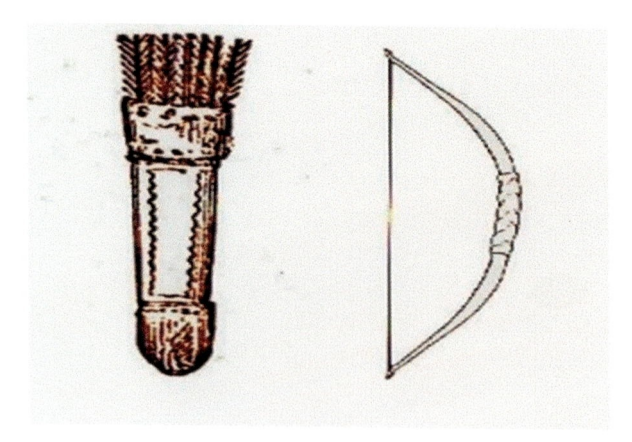

As shown in verse 3 of Chapter 27, we discover that Esau hunted with a bow and arrows. Isaac told him to take up his weapons, the quiver and bow (a quiver holds the arrows).

We see again that Esau was a hairy man and that Jacob was a smooth-skinned man (verse 11).

Back to the story.

Verses 13 and 14 describe how Esau and Jacob's mother would take the blame for Esau's action (selling his birthright), and how she schemes with Jacob to complete his acquiring of the birthright from Isaac, his father. She orders Jacob to get a young goat so that she can cook a savory meal of meat for Isaac. She instructs Jacob to take the cooked meat to his father who is lying in his tent.

V15: And Rebekah took goodly raiment of her elder son Esau, which were with her in the house, and put them upon Jacob her younger son:

V16: And she put the skins of the kids of the goats upon his hands, and upon the smooth of his neck:

Break

Verse 16 gives us some insight into what type of body hair covered Esau. When reading the story of Esau, we naturally think of Esau's body hair as the same as the hair on our bodies but thicker. However, in verse 16 we can see that the body hair that covered Esau's body was a lot different than our hair.

Esau's body was covered with hair like thick fur; it was far from the familiar body hair we have today.

V17: And she gave the savory meat and bread which she had prepared, into the hands of her son Jacob.

V18: And he came unto his father, and said, My father: and he said, Here am I; how art thou, my son?

V19: And Jacob said unto his father, I am Esau thy firstborn; I have done according as thou badest me: arise I pray thee, sit and eat of my venison, that thy soul may bless me.

V20: And Isaac said unto his son, How is it that thou hast found it so quickly, my son? And he said, Because the Lord thy God brought it to me.

V21: And Isaac said unto Jacob, Come near, I pray thee, that I may feel thee, my son, whether thou be my very son Esau or not.

V22: And Jacob went near unto Isaac his father; and he felt him, and said, The voice is Jacob's voice, but the hands are the hands of Esau.

V23: And he discerned him not, because his hands were hairy, as his brother Esau's hands: And he said, I am.

V24: And he said, Art thou my very son Esau? And he said, I am.

V25: And he said, Bring it near to me, and I will eat of my son's venison, that my soul may bless thee. And he brought it near to him, and he did eat: and he brought him wine, and he drank.

V26: And his father Isaac said unto him, Come near now, and kiss me, my son.

V27: And he came near, and kissed him: and he smelled the smell of his raiment, and blessed him, and said, See the smell of my son is as the smell of a field which the Lord hath blessed:

Break

When Isaac was old he lost his sight. The only way he could tell his sons apart was by feeling, smelling, and hearing their voice. However, when Esau's mother placed his clothes on Jacob along with the kid's (goat) hair, the only difference that Isaac noticed was the voice.

Nevertheless, because he recognized the feel and smell as Esau, he gave Jacob the blessing.

Verses 28 through 29 describe the blessing he gave to Jacob. It isn't until verses 30 and 31 that we see Esau come back from the hunt to bring the savory meat to his father.

Back to the story

V32: And Isaac his father said unto him, Who art thou? And he said, I am thy son thy first-born Esau.

V33: And Isaac trembled very exceedingly, and said, Who? Where is he that hath taken venison, and brought it me, and I have eaten of all before thou camest, and have blessed him? Yea, and he shall be blessed.

V34: And when Esau heard the words of his father, he cried with a great and exceeding bitter cry, and said unto his father, Bless me, even me also, O my father.

Break

Esau was angry when he found out about his brother's trickery; as it is told, Esau let out a bitter cry for what Jacob had done to him. The story of Esau is told throughout the Bible in different contexts. The blessing Isaac give Esau was he was to live off of the fat of the land and drink from the waters of the heavens.

The story of Esau tells us that Esau was the first Edomite; his name was changed when he sold his birthright to his brother Jacob. Esau had five wives and his descendants lived in the city of Edom.

Here is three of Esau's wives.

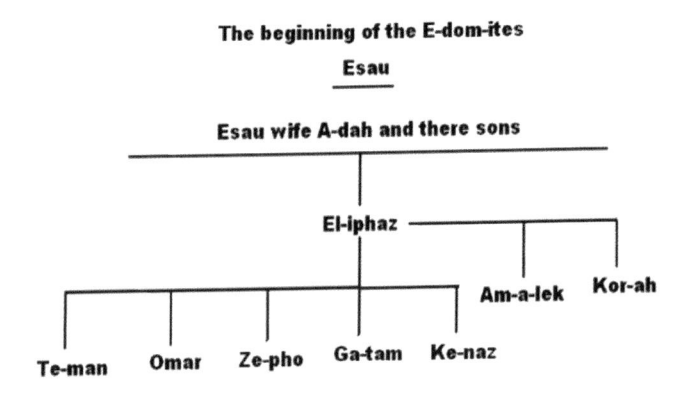

The beginning of the E-dom-ites

Esau

Esau wife A-dah and there sons

- El-iphaz
  - Te-man
  - Omar
  - Ze-pho
  - Ga-tam
  - Ke-naz
  - Am-a-lek
  - Kor-ah

Esau's first wife had sons by Esau, but she also had sons by her own sons as well.

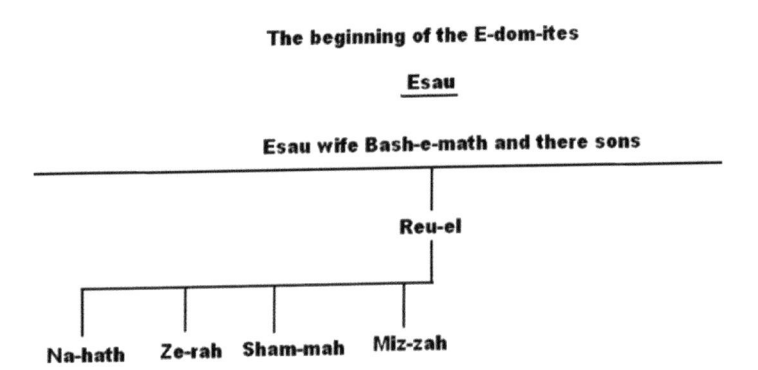

The beginning of the E-dom-ites

Esau

Esau wife Bash-e-math and there sons

- Reu-el
  - Na-hath
  - Ze-rah
  - Sham-mah
  - Miz-zah

Esau's second wife also had sons by Esau and by her own sons.

The beginning of the E-dom-ites

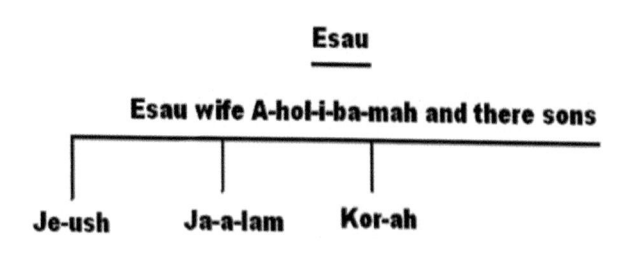

Esau

Esau wife A-hol-i-ba-mah and there sons

| Je-ush | Ja-a-lam | Kor-ah |

Esau's last wife Aholibamah only had sons by Esau. She was the only wife Esau had that did not procreate with her sons.

Esau was the start of a new breed of man. This type of man was to be stronger and bigger than normal men. And this new man had fur-like hair that covered its body. This is why Esau's wives had sons by their own sons because their sons by Esau looked different than all the other men of that time. The wives' sons had fur-like hair covering their bodies and this abnormal trait made it hard for their sons to get wives. Esau's wives also had females born unto them. The sons of Esau took their sisters and cousins for wives. Thus, incest was practiced in the family of Esau.

This was the start of the Edomites. They lived in Edom. However, over 3,000 years ago, the Romans went to

Edom to kill all the males in the city because they were afraid of this type of man. After the Romans killed most of the males living in Edom at the time, the Romans departed. Some Edomites who managed to flee later returned. When they saw the devastation wrought by Rome, they abandoned their city and were never seen again. Then when the Romans knew they had left females still alive, they marched back to Edom to kill the females, but the females were gone.

Around the same time the Edomites left Edom, the first reports of the Yeti were reported in Asia. When the Edomites left Edom to save themselves, they traveled eastward from Edom. This was the start of the whole story of the Yeti.

In my investigation of the story of Esau, the description of Esau as told in the Bible matched the man I saw in 2002. Most interestingly, centuries ago the famous artist

Michelangelo studied the stories of the Bible; and what is most fascinating, he created a painting of the hairy man of Edom.

The Judgment

Michelangelo's most famous painting resides on the dome of the Sistine Chapel in Vatican City, Rome.

In the painting, Michelangelo took scenes from Bible stories and placed them together. As you can see, at the bottom of the painting, the Edomites were cast out by man.

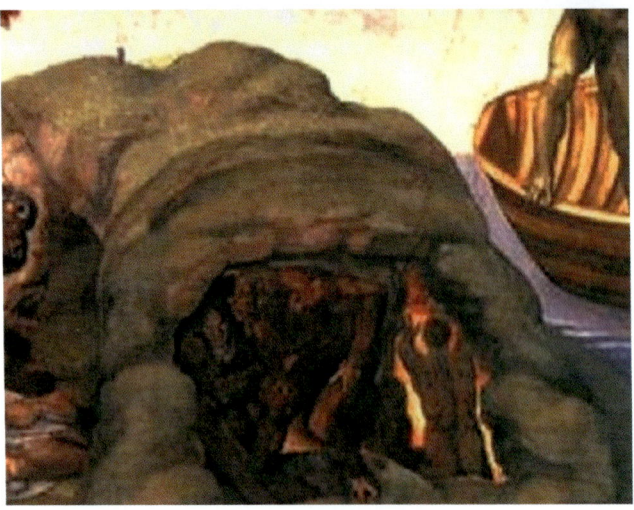

In this close up, we see the man casting out the Edomites so that normal man could live in the caves.

This is one of the first images in history that shows what the Edomites looked like as described in the Bible. Although the Bible is the earliest source for the existence of this type of "man of the woods," there is a lot more evidence out there that supports the existence of the Edomites.

Edom is where the Edomites lived.

They lived in cave cities they built.

In the United States and other locations around the world, we see these same types of cave cities. I have been working in construction for 33 years and am very familiar with the design and construction of buildings and other structures. There are many similarities between the city of Edom and other cave cities found in the United States and other countries. Could those who built Edom have built other cave cities around the world? These cave cities share the same or very similar styles and workmanship.

In Utah there is a rock called The Newspaper Rock. On this rock there is drawing that tells different stories from years past.

In this image of the rock we can see different types of drawings, but the most curious images that stand out the most are the big creatures with horns on their heads and the big foot prints. We can interpret ancient drawings in many ways, but there is something that stands out in these drawing that tell a story of the native Indians. The creatures with horns appear to have taught the Indians to hunt with the bow—and to track. Another story is in the images: why the creatures with horns came to America.

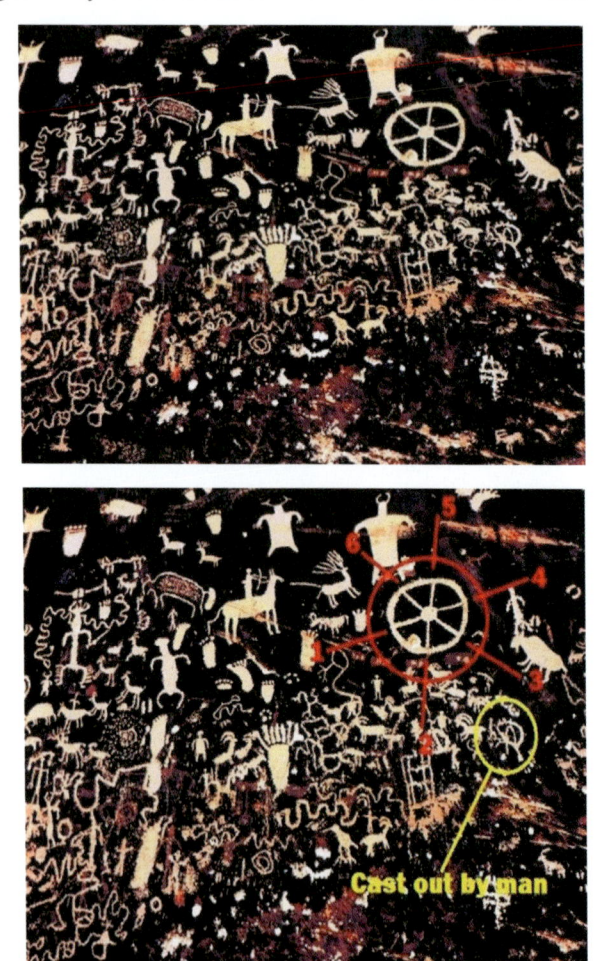

Cast out by man

On this rock a man is casting out the creatures. And the wheel that is on this rock seems to have special significance.

You would think this was simply an old wagon wheel, but there are 12 to 14 spokes on a wagon wheel. The drawing shows a wagon wheel with only 6 spokes.

The only wheel we know of is a war chariot wheel—it had six spokes. As the Bible tells us, the Romans marched on Edom to destroy all the male Edomites. The Romans left and later traveled back to kill all the

Edomite females; but they were gone. The Romans had war chariots. The wheel shown on the rock suggests a wheel of one of the Roman war chariots. Native Indians would not have known about the Romans or of the chariots of war. Perhaps the images on the rock depict the story of the Edomites, a story passed on by the Edomites themselves to the Native Indians.

The cave cities date back to over 2,000 years. The newspaper rock shown in this story looks like it dates back to about 1,000 years, perhaps longer. The British did not come to this land the Thirteen Colonies until only a few hundred years ago.

On this rock there are a lot of stories, but it is hard to find out what story was on the rock first and the order of the stories. It turns out the stories on the rock were added as years passed by. The first stories told on the rock were lost as the years passed. As more stories were added, some of the newer stories overlaid earlier stories. The only way to draw any conclusions is to point out some facts that can be seen on the rock, namely, the man casting out a creature to live in caves, the chariot wheel, and hunting with the bow. These images can be seen, but placing them at the same time is difficult, if not impossible.

The Native Indians knew of this type of man for more than a thousand years, and the Edomites found peace with the Indians. They lived together, and the Edomites helped build the cities in the sides of the mountains.

They also taught the Indians skills, notably hunting with the bow and tracking.

Cave drawings in Edom

Edomites money

Cave drawings in the USA

This image shows the type of money used in Edom and the drawings found in the caves of ancient Edom. The drawings are the same types of drawings found in Indian caves in the United States.

35

Here is another cave drawing that again shows a creature.

A lot of evidence exists at different locations in the world of cave drawings and Bigfoot tracks on rocks. A most curious find are modern government maps that have symbols of Bigfoot creatures on them.

36

This is a military training map discovered by MK Davis.

On this military map, we see a picture of a Sasquatch. The unique design of the Sasquatch/Bigfoot image dates the map to the 1970s. Also, the words "Big Foot" did not come into broad popular usage until the early 1960s. It wasn't until the mid-1950s that Bigfoot (often used as two words) began to appear in various newspapers. If not the 1970s, the map was possibly produced later than 1960.

Unless this map is a joke, the US government appears to have accepted a real Bigfoot existing on forest land.

37

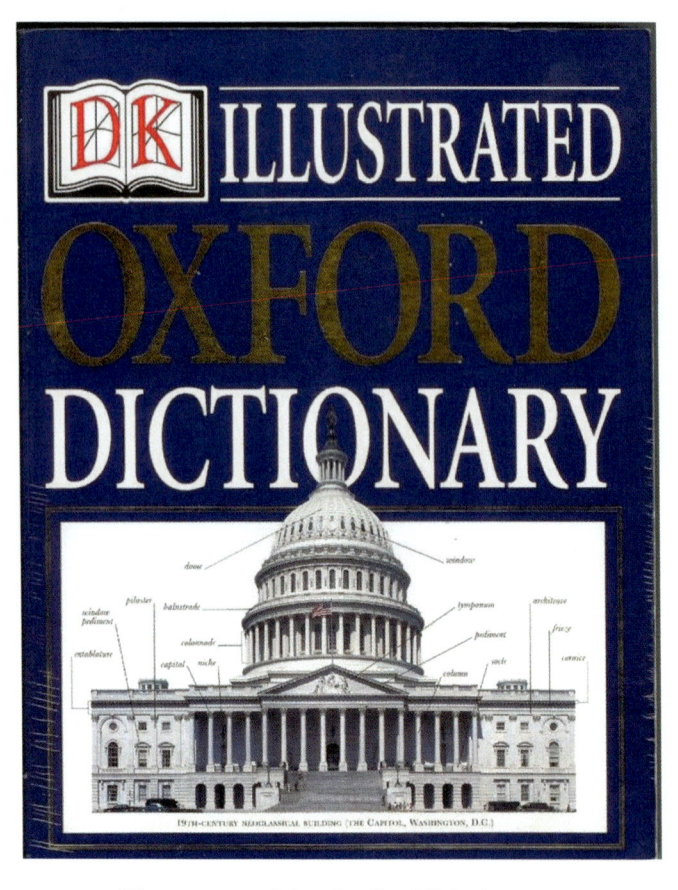

The cover of the Oxford Dictionary.

The date published 09/15/1998 edition of the Oxford Dictionary accepts Bigfoot as a word defining a real creature.

Abominable Snowman

a·bom·i·na·ble /əbóminəbəl/ *adj.* **1** detestable; loathsome. **2** *colloq.* very bad or unpleasant (*abominable weather*). □□ **a·bom·i·na·bly** *adv.*

a·bom·i·na·ble snow·man *n.* a humanoid or bear-like animal said to exist in the Himalayas; a yeti.

a·bom·i·nate /əbóminayt/ *v.tr.* detest; loathe.

Yeti

yet·i /yétee/ n. = ABOMINABLE SNOWMAN.

Sasquatch

Sask. *abbr.* Saskatchewan.
Sas·quatch /sáskwoch, -kwach/ *n.* a supposed yeti-like animal of NW America. Also called **Bigfoot**.
sass /sas/ *n. & v. colloq.* ● *n.* impudence, disrespectful mannerism or speech. ● *v.tr.* be

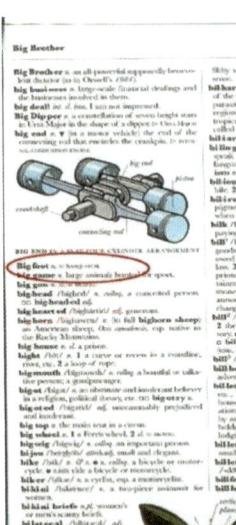

Bigfoot

BIG END IN A FLAT FOUR CYLINDER ARRANGEMENT

Big·foot *n.* = SASQUATCH.

big game *n.* large animals hunted for sport.

The Oxford Dictionary also contains the words Abominable Snowman, Yeti, and Sasquatch.

In summary: The Holy Bible describes a type of man with fur covering his body. The city this man lived in with his family is like similar cities in the US and other countries. The cave drawings found in the US match the cave drawings in Edom. The government marks the existence of this type of man in forests on their maps. The Native Indians have numerous tales about this kind of man. Thousands of sighting reports have been compiled; some extend back as far as 3,000 years. Thousands of people have found tracks over the years. I had a first-hand observation, face to face in 2002. The stories I have read and the reports I have studied convince me that what I saw in 2002 is the same as so many other Bigfoots reported over decades.

With 90% of the reports claiming observations of a big hairy man, then Bigfoot is most likely a type of man. My interpretation of the data is that witnesses are seeing not a creature nor an animal, but as the witnesses claim, a hairy man, in short, a hairy man from Biblical times, a descendant of the Edomites.

For years, people have attached a variety of names to these hairy men. For example, in the first image to the left witnesses called him the Dog Man. My contention is that such men have the same genes as did Esau and the Edomite descendants. Thousands of years ago, the Edomites procreated with smooth-skin people. These "Dog Men" in the image above are their descendants.

My second encounter.

My first Bigfoot encounter happened in 2002 when I saw a real live Bigfoot face to face. Later, I had a second encounter, not a sighting, but strong evidence that my wife and I were of interest to one of these hairy men, a Bigfoot.

In the summer of 2012, I and my wife **were** sitting in the living room. I was working at my computer going over some Bigfoot films and doing some research on JFK (another of my many projects). My wife was reading a book. It was around 2:00 in the morning and it was a hot night, but a storm had come through in the late evening. We had the windows open to get some air. Suddenly, we both heard a loud sound outside by the river. I stepped outside out and looked around in the rain, but I did not see anything. However, there was a smell in the air that I had smelled before when I experienced my encounter in 2002, but I couldn't see anything this night that could have caused the smell.

After going back in the house, my wife asked what had caused the noise. I told her I didn't know. She told me to close the window: "There's a skunk outside and it smells bad." I closed the window and continued to work, listening to the storm. My wife returned to her reading. When the storm ended and the inside air cooled, we closed the windows and went to bed.

The next morning as I opened the window to get some cool air, I pulled down the screen, my eyes fell on what appeared to be an imprint of a face on the window. I immediately photographed it.

After I took this image, as you can see, nothing is apparently visible. I asked my nephew take a black sheet outside and cover the back of the window. I then took another picture.

Image of the window backed with a black sheet.

Evident are a face and fingerprints.

Inverting the image on the window revealed more details.

After inverting the image, close-up shots bring out even more detail.

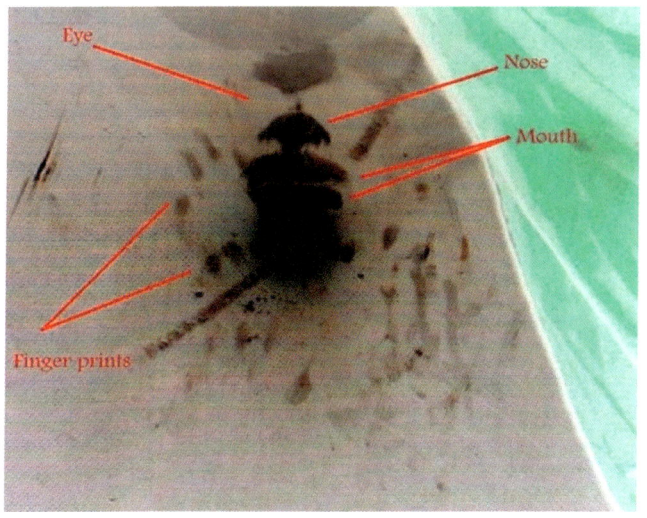

In the close-up above, one can see that there was something looking in on me and my wife! Inspection shows the outline of two eyes, a mouth, a long chin, and finger prints around the side of the face. In an attempt to sample the anomalous material on the window, I noticed that dust from a nearby driveway had attached to the imprint, which prevented pristine removal of the image (such as by scraping).

However, I was confident that the photographs proved that something had pressed itself against the glass pane to look closely in on me and my wife. If a person, it was an unusual being with big eyes, prominent lips, and a long chin.

I also discovered a Bigfoot track near the window and took photographs of it. Unfortunately, the digital images were destroyed when I accidentally dropped a flash drive that held the photographs into a glass of water next to my computer!

The track was nine inches wide and twenty-one inches long. I concluded that the face on the window was from a juvenile Bigfoot. The face was large but not of adult size.

Something to think about:

Researchers have been trying to prove the existence of this type of man for years, but evidence of its existence has been all around us, if we look, for thousands of years. If someone one day finds, captures, and detains one of these beings for all to see and study—and if it is determined the being is of human origin, what will happen? That is, wouldn't this strange, hairy man have to respect man's laws? Wouldn't it need to learn new behaviors? Would such an anomalous man be capable of changing the way it lived? I would have to answer, No.

Let me explain:

Let us say there are about 20,000 of these Bigfoot people in the world; and let us assume all are proved to be human, although unusual in appearance. Wouldn't we wish to domesticate them? We would do this from good intentions, to improve their lives, to prevent their premature deaths at the hands of violent nature and wild predators. They might have survived in the wilds, but how far had they advanced? We would wish to see their lives improved. Slowly, they could be integrated fully into our society and join the world community. Naturally, we would wish them to live in houses, not in forests and caves. Lawfully, we would demand that they have a roof over their heads. The men would become the head of their family; their women would become mothers living in houses with electricity and running water. All well and good, yet societies still suffer to one degree or another from racism. Would "normal" humans want to live next to a family of Bigfoot, their children go to school and work next to them?

As Bigfoot researchers, there are many issues to consider beyond capturing a live Bigfoot. For example, I often think, are we out to prove the existence of Bigfoot, or is our search merely to inflate our egos, to convince people around us that we are extremely smart, that we are on the leading edge of a new science? For me, I am more interested in proving for myself that this type of man does in fact exists. I saw one. I don't need to hunt for Bigfoot.

Therefore, I pose many questions that require answers should one of these hairy men be found alive. What would happen if a family of them was captured and the government stepped in and took the family away and performed hurtful tests on them? Remember, for every new species of flora and fauna found on earth, there is always someone who will test, dissect, and destroy to gather knowledge of the structure, organization, functioning, and genetic make-up of the new species— all from the desire to advance science and to gain the accolades of the scientific community, or for sheer profit (witness the sad story of the gorilla in the movie *King Kong*).

Remember, I saw one of these men face to face. I could see into its eyes; he was a man—yes, a strange one—yet a man with likely a family that needed his support. Was he hunting the day I came upon him? Like most men, was he doing what he could do for his family? I am certain this "man" has feelings the same as we do.

Just something to think about.

Shown above are two test images I produced. I keep these images on file when I study films or images of Bigfoot. These two test images do not show a real Bigfoot. Rather, they show me—well, me inside a

51

Bigfoot suit that I constructed when I examined the Patterson and Gimlin (P/G) Bigfoot film.

I show these images to people as examples of hoax images of Bigfoot, because unfortunately there are many so-called "Bigfoot investigators" trying to make a name for themselves; or more likely make money off fake Bigfoot images or films.

In the past 20 years there have been more hoaxes in the Bigfoot field than any time in the past. Therefore, in all the films and images I analyze, I look for tell-tale clues that unmask the purported "evidence" as a lie.

The 1967 P/G Bigfoot film has been studied for (as of this writing) nearly 50 years. There is only one other film that has been viewed more, the Abraham Zapruder film of the JFK Assassination on November 22, 1963.

The Bigfoot research world considers the P/G film as the Holy Grail of Bigfoot "evidence"—the first real Bigfoot ever filmed.

However, in the last nearly 50 years, there have been numerous stories and intriguing evidence that disprove the authenticity of the film.

To find the truth, I decided to collect and closely examine all the stories and overlooked facts to answer the question: Is the P/G film fiction or non-fiction? You'll be surprised at what I found.

Chapter Two: The Story

Here is the basic story that has been told of the famous Patterson and Gimlin Bigfoot film. I first present each element and/or fact, and then point out what simply doesn't add up.

The Story:

In September of 1967, Roger Patterson talked to Bob Gimlin about traveling to Mount St. Helens to look for a Bigfoot. After Bob Gimlin made arrangements, he and Roger headed out to Mount St. Helens.

When they arrived, Roger started to talk to Bob about going on expeditions with him to look for Bigfoot. Roger told Bob about some of the eyewitness accounts and played tapes from eyewitnesses. After about a week, both Roger and Bob returned to their home town of Yakima, Washington.

When Roger got back home, he received a phone call from John Green, one of the "wise men" of Bigfoot studies, claiming that he and fellow investigators had just got back from Blue Creek Mountain where they found fresh Bigfoot tracks. After the call came in, Roger drove to Bob Gimlin's home and asked him to take him down to Blue Creek Mountain in California.

Note:

This phone call places John Green in the Blue Creek mountains in the month of September.

After Roger talked to Bob, Bob took some time off of work and made arrangements. They both loaded up horses and headed down to the Blue Creek Mountain area.

They arrived in Bluff Creek, California, around the last week of September or the first week of October. After the passage of about two weeks, Bob told Roger that he had to get back home because of work. Roger then asked Bob to just give him a few more days, and if they didn't find anything they would head back home.

Note:

Because Roger and Bob arrived in the Bluff Creek area the last week of September or the first week of October, Roger and Bob were in the Bluff Creek area for around 20 to 27 days.

Back to the story:

Then on Friday, October 20, 1967, Bob got up early, saddled his horse, and rode out looking around while Roger slept in. As Bob was riding horseback, his horse threw a shoe so Bob decided to head back to camp to re-shoe the horse. When Bob returned to camp, Roger was gone. Bob re-shoed the horse; then Roger returned back at camp.

Note:

Where was Roger Patterson when Bob return back to camp? We are never told.

54

Back to the story:

After Roger and Bob ate breakfast, they started out on horseback. When Bob tried to go to different locations, Roger told Bob to go back to the location where they were the day before. As they were riding through the forest, Roger started filming the landscape.

About 1:30 PM after riding around, the men started to ride up stream of Bluff Creek. As they made a turn around a downed tree that had fallen across the creek bed, they looked over to their left; and there sitting in a squat-down position was some kind of "creature."

As their horses started to buck, Roger and Bob tried to keep the horses under control. Roger and his horse fell to the ground with Roger's horse right on top of him. Roger then got up and grabbed his camera out of the saddle bag and started to run toward the creature while filming it. When Roger started to film, the creature stood up on two legs and started to walk away. Then, as Bob was trying to control his horse and the pack horse, Roger yelled for Bob to cover him. Bob let the pack horse go and rode across the creek bed and pulled out his rifle from the holster and covered Roger.

When Roger ran across the creek bed filming the creature, he fell down and got back up as the creature just walked away. Then when Roger got to a level location in the creek bed, the creature looked back at Roger or Bob. Both men claim that the Bigfoot was looking at them. Then, as the creature walked away and

Roger continued to film it, the creature walked away behind logs that **were** piled up along the creek bed.

Note:

What took place after the creature left is unclear. First, Roger and Bob stayed at the filming location. But as years passed by the story changed, and Bob took off on his horse after the creature up the hillside to the dirt road above Bluff Creek. Then Bob heard Roger calling for him and he returned to the film site. Later, Roger and Bob claimed that after they found their horses (they had bolted in the excitement), both Roger and Bob followed the Bigfoot's tracks up the hillside and down a dirt road, which they followed for about 2 miles. Then, they returned to the film site.

In another version of this part of the story, the Bigfoot made a turn when it was behind the stacked logs and took off running.

Why did the Bigfoot at first just walk away, but later it started to run away?

Back to the story:

After the creature left, Roger and Bob gathered the horses up, and Roger took out a rain poncho and covered himself with it. He then changed the film in the camera—the camera had run out of film as he was filming the creature. Soon after Roger changed the film, he shot more film of the tracks and did a test with Bob jumping down on the sand in the creek bed to estimate the weight of the creature.

Note:

If Roger's horse and the packhorse ran away during the excitement, how did Roger and Bob find them? How long did it take for them to find the horses?

Back to the story:

Roger and Bob rode back to the camp site and got some plaster out of the truck. They rode back to the film site and made some cast prints from the tracks the creature made in the sand. When they were making the cast prints, they filmed some more. Soon after they finished filming, making the cast prints, performing the weight test, and taking measurements of the prints and stride, they headed back to camp. They fed the horses and drove the truck out of Bluff Creek, leaving all their camping gear and horses at the camp site as they drove to Eureka to air mail the film to Seattle Washington so that Roger's brother-in-law Al DeAtley could pick it up and get it developed.

After sending out the film, the men drove back to the town of Willow Creek to Al Hodgson's store to make some phone calls. They arrived about 9:00 or 9:30 PM at the store. Roger called the Times-Standard newspaper about what he just filmed and then made some calls to other people.

Note:

In the story told by Roger Patterson and Bob Gimlin they claimed to have gone down to Eureka Ca. to air mail the film out. Then they drove back to Willow Creek and then called Times-Standard newspaper that is located in Eureka Ca. to have an interview over the phone. But if Roger and Bob was already in Eureka Ca. to air mail the film out then why they did not stop by Times- Standard newspaper office and give their story?

Back to the story:

As Roger was making the calls, Bob found some boxes to take back to the film site to cover the creature's tracks. Then, soon after the phone calls were made and Roger was interviewed at the Times-Standard newspaper, Roger and Bob headed back to the camp site.

Note 1:

Roger and Bob only had eight hours to film the Bigfoot, do their weight test and make casts of the tracks, do more filming, find their horses, and then ride back and forth to the campsite and film site, then drive all the way to Eureka to air mail the film to Seattle, Washington and drive back to Willow Creek. Plus, they left their camping gear and horses out in the open all alone without anyone watching the horses or gear.

Note 2:

When Roger was making calls on what he and Bob had just filmed, Jim McClarin, a Northern California Bigfoot investigator, also made a call to cryptozoologist Ivan Sanderson about Roger filming a female Bigfoot at Bluff Creek.

Back to the story:

When Roger and Bob returned to the camp site, they sat around the fire eating and talking about what they had seen that day and what they had filmed. Then, about 3:00 or 4:00 AM on October 21, 1967, it started to rain. Bob took out the cardboard boxes he got from a store in Willow Creek. He rode on horseback to the film site and tried to cover the tracks, but the boxes were too wet; so he took some bark off of the trees and tried to cover some of the tracks so they wouldn't wash away. When he got back to the camp site, the creek started to rise.

When he saw the water rising, he woke up Roger and alerted him to the danger, and they both decided to head back home. As they started home to Yakima, Jim McClarin and Rene Dahinden arrived at Willow Creek at Al Hodgson's store. They left together and drove to the location where Roger and Bob had camped, and discovered they had left. Then Jim and Rene traveled to the film site and took some photos of the Bigfoot tracks the creature had left. Soon after they took the photos, they headed back to the store in Willow Creek and found that Roger and Bob had left for home. Jim and Rene decided to head to Yakima to meet up with Roger and Bob.

Note:

If Roger and Bob were the only ones who knew the location where they filmed the Bigfoot, how did Rene and Jim know where they filmed the creature?

Back to the story:

As Roger and Bob were heading home on that Saturday, October 21, and with Rene and Jim also heading to Yakima, Roger Patterson's brother in-law Al DeAtley drove to Seattle to pick up the film at the airport around 10:30 AM. When DeAtley received the film, he went out to find a place to develop it. After finding a place that was open on Saturday and getting the film developed, he returned home to Yakima.

Note:

Where did Al DeAtley get the film developed on Saturday when most of the places that develop film were not open or they closed early on Saturdays?

To find the answer to the question, I spent 3 months contacting filming companies in and around Seattle Washington to find out if any of the companies was open on a Saturday and was open in 1967.

Then on Jan 23, 2012 I contacted a Mr. Jensen by phone that worked for Alpha Cine Labs in Seattle Washington and ask him my I contact him again by email to answer some questions for me that I may have them on file. He agreed and he gave me his email address. After I hung up the phone I then wrote him and email asking him was they open on Saturday's and what time they closed and was they open in 1967. I also asked him if they were the ones who have developed a Bigfoot film for Al DeAtly on Saturday Oct. 21, 1967.

He contacted me back on the same day and here is his reply:

Mr. Blevins:

I have spoken to some of our staff and can confirm that Alpha Cine was open 7 days a week in that time because we developed news film for all the TV stations. Reporters would drop the film off, it would be developed and returned very quickly...it needed to be used on the evening news. My operations director was not here in 1967 but knows that Alpha Cine did develop the Sasquatch Film for these people. There have been others researching this topic over the years.
I think I can answer all of your questions in the affirmative. As to closing time...it probably would have been fairly late in the evening to cover the evening news at 11pm.
Happy to respond to other questions.

Don Jensen

Alpha Cine Labs

Mr. Jensen did say in his email that they did developed the Bigfoot film and they were open on Saturday and in 1967. However, was it the P/G film they developed or was it another film? This question will never be answered because Alpha Cine Labs is no longer in business and there are no records on file to what was exactly that was on film they developed.

Back to the story:

On Sunday, October 22, 1967, the first people to arrive at Al DeAtley's home were John Green, Rene Dahinden, and Jim McClarin.

Note:

With Roger and Bob leaving the Bluff Creek area hours before Rene and Jim left Bluff Creek, how did Rene and Jim get to Al DeAtley's home before Roger and Bob?

Who called John Green and how could he be in Yakima at the same time as Rene and Jim when John Green was in British Columbia?

Back to the story:

After some time had passed, Roger and Bob arrived back in Yakima around 10:30 AM Sunday. Bob dropped off Roger at his house and Bob went home. Roger then got into his car and drove over to his brother in-law's house. When Roger arrived at Al's home, they both went down to Al's basement to view the film. After viewing the film for the first time, they asked the rest of the men upstairs to come down and view the film.

Note:

I find it odd that Al DeAtley received the film in Seattle at the airport at 10:30 AM and then just 24 hours later Roger and Bob were back in Yakima, and Patterson and DeAtley were viewing the film for the first time in DeAtley's basement, all in a short 24 hours. And Patterson now had influential Bigfoot investigators in his brother-in-law's home. These events seem well-coordinated.

Back to the story:

After viewing the film, Roger talked about where the group could set up a conference to show the film to the public. John Green advised Roger to take his time and do it right, but Roger pushed the issue.

On Monday, October 23, 1967, Roger, John Green, and Rene Dahinden took the film to British Columbia. Around 7:30 PM that night, they invited a room full of people and scientists to view two reels of film. After viewing the film with the alleged Bigfoot in it, one of the scientists claimed that the creature possessed breasts and it was a female.

Note:

In some interviews, Roger and Bob claimed they found out the creature was a female after one of the scientists pointed out the breasts on the creature at the October 23, 1967 viewing. But they also claimed they knew it was a female when they were filming the creature.

I also like to point out that in their story they claimed to have shown two reels of film but when I contacted John Green by email he gave me another story.

On Sep.18, 2010 John Green reply to another question I have asked him.

I asked him where did Al DeAtley got the film developed and what was on reel one and reel two that they show in British Columbia on Monday Oct. 23, 1963.

John Green reply:

DeAtley, whose word is not to be relied on, now claims to have forgotten where he got the film processed. He would not say at the time, indicating that he did not want to get someone in trouble. I know of only one reel developed at that time.

By John Green reply there was only one reel of film and not two reels. This again brings up another question on why at first they claimed there was two reels of film taken and shown when in fact there was only the one reel?

Back to the story:

After viewing both films, one of the scientists asked Roger for a copy of reel two so they could study it. Roger agreed to provide them with a copy of the second reel by Friday, October 27. However, Roger never kept that promise and never provided a copy of the second reel. As the years went by, the so-called second reel was never seen again; it was supposedly lost.

Note:

As it was told, the second reel of film shows Roger Patterson making cast prints and Gimlin jumping off of a log to see how deep his tracks would be in the sand of Bluff Creek. They also filmed the path the Bigfoot took when it walked away and some other miscellaneous scenes. However, no one has seen the second film since October 23, 1967. There are parts of some film in someone's hands, it is claimed, from the second reel. However, this is hearsay.

On March 29, 1992 John Green done a tape recording interview with Bob Gimlin. And on this recording they talked about the second reel of film that was show at The University of British Columbia. But as I point out from an email I received from John Green there was no second reel only the one reel that was shown at B/C but in the interview they both talked about reel two being shown.

I like to add that in that same interview of John Green and Bob Gimlin done on March 29, 1992 that Bob Gimlin claimed that it was almost dark after they was done filming and doing their test and feeding the horse. And that Roger and himself arrived at Al Hodgson story around 8:30 or 9:00 PM and there they were deciding what town to ship the film by air mail.

By the interview of Bob Gimlin by John Green the film was air mailed out way after 9:00 PM that Friday night.

And the rest is history.

After reviewing the story based on the facts I had collected, I made some notes on what to look for when viewing the film. Here are items that come to mind when only studying the story, let alone the actual film itself.

1) If the creature in the film is female, then where was the male? In the wild, a male creature does not leave a female creature alone out in the open.
2) When Roger started to run up on the Bigfoot, why did the creature simply walk away and not run? An animal perceiving a threat would immediately run. In this case, a man (Roger) with a camera was running toward the creature.

3) Roger and Bob claim they filmed the creature on a Friday afternoon, and that there were men in the area working cutting down trees. Where were these men at the time Roger filmed the creature?

4) How did the creature run down the dirt road for two miles with trucks going in and out all day long on a work day?

5) Why were there no reports of other Bigfoot tracks found after Roger filmed the Bigfoot?

The last time Bigfoot tracks were reported in the Bluff Creek area was on September 5, 1967, after Labor Day weekend. Workers in the area reported the tracks at the time. The workers even claimed that Bigfoot tracks were found in the Bluff Creek sand bed in early September.

6) With Roger and Bob in the Bluff Creek area for 20 to 27 days searching for Bigfoot, why didn't they talk to workers in the area who were working daily in the woods? No workers ever reported seeing Roger or Bob in the Bluff Creek area.

Not once did Roger and Bob ever state they talked to workers in the area or saw workers or trucks going in and out of the work area (trees were being cleared to construct a logging road). One would think that the Bigfoot "hunters" would have asked questions to ascertain where to focus their search.

7) Roger and Bob claimed their horses started to buck when they came upon the creature. However, horses would sense the creature some distance away. With Roger and Bob located downstream riding upstream, the creature would have been upwind in

the creek bed. The horses would have smelled it way before they got close to it and started to buck. Even Roger and Bob would have smelled it before they came upon it. The creature was only 80 to 90 feet away.

However, Roger, Bob, and the horses did not smell it or felt its presence until they came around the fallen tree.

My research uncovered many loose ends in Roger and Bob's story. I discovered that when someone questioned holes in their story, all Roger and Bob would say was that they forgot; or someone else would come to their aid and make up excuses for them.

Every serious researcher who has followed the PG film story has noticed that as the years go by, and the more the story is told, the more details get added to the story.

What story can we believe today?

As the story is told and re-told, the story changes and new "facts" are added; or in some cases, old facts are ignored, refuted, or retracted. The entire process does nothing but engender new questions that demand answers.

Here are some examples:

In the late 1960s and early 1970s Roger Patterson and Bob Gimlin were interviewed. In these interviews, Gimlin states that the arms of the Bigfoot hung down by its knees. Roger Patterson retorted: "Now Bob, don't exaggerate."

In the 1990s Bob Gimlin said that Roger exaggerated when he said the horse and Roger fell to the ground.

So you see, who can you believe or not believe?

When Roger and Bob said that the Bigfoot in the film was a female, at first they claimed they did not know it was a female until one of the scientists in British Columbia pointed out the breasts on the Bigfoot. But as the years went by, Roger and Bob claimed they knew it was a female as they filmed it.

In another story, Jim McClarin contacted Ivan Sanderson on Friday night, October 20, 1967, and told Sanderson that Roger Patterson just filmed a female Bigfoot. How could Roger know the Bigfoot was a female? He said he only learned this when a scientist pointed out the breasts (as noted, later Roger changes this detail of the story).

In 2010, Bob Gimlin tells a new story about Roger using a stand-in double for Gimlin when he went on the road to show the film in public venues in the late 1960s and early 1970s. Gimlin goes on to say that in a deathbed confession, Roger asked Bob to forgive him for using a stand-in double instead of Bob himself.

With this in mind, unless the stand-in double knew every detail and nuance of the PG film story, the double would have given false statements—the real Bob Gimlin wasn't even present at the public showings!

The only way to find out the true story of what took place the day Roger Patterson and Bob Gimlin filmed an alleged real Bigfoot is to study the very first interview that Roger Patterson and Bob Gimlin gave.

Mrs. Bigfoot Is Filmed!

A YAKIMA, WASH. man and his Indian tracking aide came out of the wilds of northern Humboldt county yesterday to breathlessly report that they had seen and taken motion pictures of "a giant humanoid creature."

In colloquial words — they have seen "Bigfoot!"

Thus, the long-sought answer to the validity and reality of the stories about the makers of the unusually large tracks lie in the some 20 to 30 feet of colored film taken by a man who has been eight years himself seeking the answer.

And as Roger Patterson spoke to The Times-Standard last night, his film was already on its way by plane to his hometown for processing while he was beside himself relating the chain of events.

Patterson, 34, has been eight years on the project. Last year he wrote a book, "Do Abominable Snowmen of America Really Exist?" This year he has been taking films of tracks and other evidence all over the Northwestern United States and Canada for a documentary.

He has over 50 tapes of interviews with persons who have reported these findings, and including talks with two or three persons who have reported seeing these giant creatures.

- o -

BOB GIMLIN, 36, and a quarter Apache Indian and also of Yakima, has been associated with Patterson for a year. Patterson has visited the area before and last month received word of the latest discovery of the giant footprints which have become legend.

Last Saturday they arrived to look for the tracks themselves and to take some films of these, riding over the mountainous terrain on horseback by day and motoring over the roads and trails by night.

Yesterday they were in the Bluff Creek area, some 65 to 70 miles north of Willow Creek, where Notice Creek comes into it. They were some two miles into a canyon where it begins to flare out.

Patterson was still an excited man some eight hours after his experience. His words came cascading out between gasps. He still couldn't believe what he had seen, but he is convinced he has now seen a "Bigfoot" himself and he's the only man he's heard of who has taken pictures of the creature.

Here is what he reported:

- o -

IT WAS about 1:30 p.m., the daylight was good, when he and Gimlin were riding their horses over a sand bar where they had been just two days before. They had both just come around a bend when "I guess we both saw it at the same time.

"I yelled 'Bob Lookit' and there about 80 or 90 feet in front of us this giant humanoid creature stood up. My horse reared and fell, completely flattening a stirrup with my foot caught in it.

(Continued on Page 2)

Front page of the *Times-Standard*, October 21, 1967

70

Bigfoot

(Continued From Page 1)

"My foot hurt but I couldn't think about it because I was jumping up and grabbing the reins to try to control the horse. I saw my camera in the saddle bag and grabbed it out, but I finally couldn't control the horse anymore and had to let him go."

- 0 -

GIMLIN was astride an older horse which is generally trail-wise, but it too rared and had to be released, running off to join their pack horse which had broken during the initial moments of the sighting.

Patterson said the creature stood upright the entire time, reaching a height of about six and a half to seven feet and an estimated weight of between 350 and 400 pounds.

"I moved to take the pictures and told Bob to cover me. My gun was still in the scabbard. I'd grabbed the camera instead. Besides, we'd made a pact not to kill one if we saw one unless we had to."

Patterson said the creatures' head was much like a human's though considerably more slated and with a large forehead and broad, wide nostrils.

"It's arms hung almost to its knees and when it walked, the arms swung at its sides."

- 0 -

PATTERSON said he is very much certain the creature was female "because when it turned toward us for a moment, I could see its breasts hanging down and they flopped when it moved."

The creature had what he described as silvery brown hair all over its body except on its face around the nose and cheeks. The hair was two to four inches long and of a light tint on top with a deeper color underneath.

"She never made a sound. She wasn't hostile to us, but we don't think she was afraid of us either. She acted like she didn't want anything to do with us if she could avoid it."

Patterson said the creature had an ambling gait as it made off over the some 200 yards he had it in sight. He said he lost sight of the creature, but Gimlin caught a brief glimpse of it afterward.

"But she stunk, like did you ever let in a dog out of the rain and he smelled like he'd been rolling in something dead. Her odor didn't last long where she'd been."

- 0 -

LATE LAST NIGHT Patterson was anxious to return to the campsite where they had left their horses. He had been to Eureka in the afternoon to airmail his film to partner Al De Atley in Yakima. De Atley has helped finance Patterson's expeditions.

He and Gimlin were equally anxious to return to the primitive area. "It's right in the middle of the primitive area" for the chance to get another view and more film of the creature.

He said there's strong belief that a family of these creatures may be in the area since footprints of 17, 15 and nine inches have been reported found.

The writer jested that these sizes put him in mind of the story of The Three Bears.

"This was no bear," Patterson said. "We have seen a lot of bears in our travels. We have seen some bears on this trip. This definitely was no bear."

Patterson is also anxious today to telephone his experience to a museum administrator who is also extremely interested in the project. "He may want to bring down some dogs. We don't have dogs here."

He's not sure how much longer they will remain in the area. "It all depends."

Page two of the *Times-Standard*, October 21, 1967

The *Times-Standard* published the very first interview of Roger Patterson and Bob Gimlin on October 21, 1967. The interview took place on Friday October 20, 1967 on the evening by phone from Al Hodgson store, the same day Patterson filmed the Bigfoot.

Mrs. Bigfoot Is Filmed!

In fact, the headline states that Roger Patterson filmed a female Bigfoot. Even in the article, Roger keeps pointing out that he and Gimlin filmed a female Bigfoot. Therefore, supposedly Roger and Bob knew it was a female Bigfoot when they filmed it.

Date they arrived was Saturday Oct 14, 1967

Female Bigfoot

Time they filmed the creature 1:30 pm

In the traditional P/G film story that has been passed down for nearly 50 years, Patterson and Gimlin say they arrived in the Bluff Creek area the last week of September or the first week of October. But in this first newspaper interview, they claim they arrived in the Bluff Creek area "last Saturday"—that would be October 14, 1967. That date would put Roger and Bob in Bluff Creek for a total time of seven days, not weeks as they claimed later. What only has remained essentially consistent in their story is the time they filmed the Bigfoot: 1:30 PM.

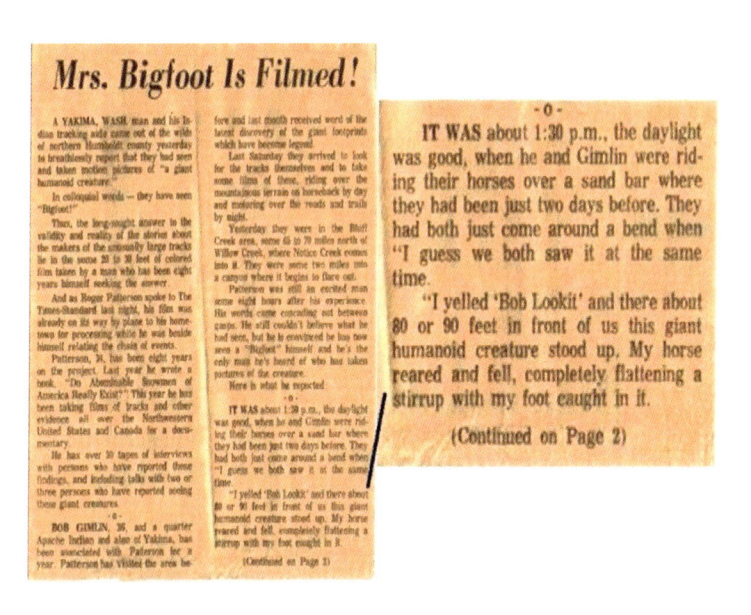

Mrs. Bigfoot Is Filmed!

A YAKIMA, WASH. man and his Indian tracking aide came out of the wilds of northern Humboldt county yesterday to breathlessly report that they had seen and taken motion pictures of "a giant humanoid creature."

In colloquial words — they have seen "Bigfoot!"

Thus, the long-sought answer to the validity and reality of the stories about the makers of the unusually large tracks lie in the some 20 to 30 feet of colored film taken by a man who has been eight years himself seeking the answer.

And as Roger Patterson spoke to The Times-Standard last night, his film was already on its way by plane to his hometown for processing while he was beside himself relating the chain of events.

Patterson, 31, has been eight years on the project. Last year he wrote a book, "Do Abominable Snowmen of America Really Exist?" This year he has been taking films of tracks and other evidence all over the Northwestern United States and Canada for a documentary.

He has over 30 tapes of interviews with persons who have reported these findings, and including talks with two or three persons who have reported seeing these giant creatures.

- o -

BOB GIMLIN, 36, and a quarter Apache Indian and also of Yakima, has been associated with Patterson for a year. Patterson has visited the area before and last month received word of the latest discovery of the giant footprints which have become legend.

Last Saturday they arrived to look for the tracks themselves and to take some films of these, riding over the mountainous terrain on horseback by day and motoring over the roads and trails by night.

Yesterday they were in the Bluff Creek area, some 65 to 70 miles north of Willow Creek, where Notice Creek comes into it. They were some two miles into a canyon where it begins to flare out.

Patterson was still an excited man some eight hours after his experience. His worth came concealing out between cards. He still couldn't believe what he had seen, but he is convinced he has now seen a "Bigfoot" himself and he's the only man he's heard of who has taken pictures of the creature.

Here is what he reported:

- o -

IT WAS about 1:30 p.m., the daylight was good, when he and Gimlin were riding their horses over a sand bar where they had been just two days before. They had both just come around a bend when "I guess we both saw it at the same time.

"I yelled 'Bob Lookit' and there about 80 or 90 feet in front of us this giant humanoid creature stood up. My horse reared and fell, completely flattening a stirrup with my foot caught in it.

(Continued on Page 2)

Page one where Roger talks about the horse he was on when it fell on him. Bob Gimlin said in a 1990s

73

interview with John Green that Roger and the horse did not fall to the ground as Roger claimed.

Bigfoot

(Continued From Page 1)

"My foot hurt but I couldn't think about it because I was jumping up and grabbing the reins to try to control the horse. I saw my camera in the saddle bag and grabbed it out, but I finally couldn't control the horse anymore and had to let him go."

- o -

GIMLIN was astride an older horse which is generally trail-wise, but it too rared and had to be released, running off to join their pack horse which had broken during the initial moments of the sighting.

Patterson said the creature stood upright the entire time, reaching a height of about six and a half to seven feet and an estimated weight of between 350 and 400 pounds.

"I moved to take the pictures and told Bob to cover me. My gun was still in the scabbard. I'd grabbed the camera instead. Besides, we'd made a pact not to kill one if we saw one unless we had to."

Patterson said the creatures' head was much like a human's, though considerably more slated and with a large forehead and broad, wide nostrils.

"It's arms hung almost to its knees and when it walked, the arms swung at its sides."

On page two Patterson finishes his story and says he let his horse go.

Bigfoot

(Continued From Page 1)

"My foot hurt but I couldn't think about it because I was jumping up and grabbing the reins to try to control the horse. I saw my camera in the saddle bag and grabbed it out, but I finally couldn't control the horse anymore and had to let him go."

GIMLIN was astride an older horse which is generally trailwise, but it too rared and had to be released, running off to join their pack horse which had broken during the initial moments of the sighting.

Patterson said the creature stood upright the entire time, reaching a height of about six and a half to seven feet and an estimated weight of between 350 and 400 pounds.

"I moved to take the pictures and told Bob to cover me. My gun was still in the scabbard. I'd grabbed the camera instead. Besides, we'd made a pact not to kill one if we saw one unless

In this part of the interview, Gimlin states that he let his horse run off with the pack horse.

What does this first public interview reveal?

Here we have Roger Patterson without his horse (it ran away in the ruckus), and, of course, the story goes that Bob Gimlin's horse also ran away. So how could Bob ride across the creek bed and yank his rifle out of the holster?

Then there is Roger Patterson's book.

In 1966 Patterson published a book entitled *Do Abominable Snowmen of America Really Exist?* I uncovered even more incriminating details in this book that cast a dark shadow over the truthfulness of the P/G film story.

> even the dust at our feet seemed to spring alive with every step. A feeling gripped me different from any I had ever experienced as my partner and I trudged our way up an old logging road on that eventful October day. It was something I hadn't felt on my first deer hunt or as I stepped into the ring to meet a tough fighter or even when the whistle blew to start the most important football game of the season. Even as we rounded a bend in the road and looked out over a wondrous land of beauty, I couldn't help but

In one part of a tale Roger sets forth in his book, he describes himself (Roger Patterson) riding horseback with his partner (No name is mentioned) down an old dirt road. *And it is October.* The story goes on to say that he and his partner came around a *bend in the road.* (At Bluff Creek, Patterson and Gimlin rode on horseback down an old dirt road and came around a *bend in the road.*) This story took place in the Bluff Creek area.

The more I re-read this story, the more convinced I became that Roger Patterson was describing in his 1966 book the actions he intended to take when he traveled with Gimlin to Bluff Creek the following year.

> About this time I realized the need for someone skilled in the art of tracking. I had thought of many prospects to fill that need but hadn't come up with anyone definite. Then one night I was down to a friend's place, Bob Gimlan, who is a quarter Apache Indian. I knew Bob spent a good deal of time in the mountains and had done much tracking of his own for wild game, and as we talked over the Bigfoot situation, Bob said he would be delighted to try his hand at helping us track these giants. At that time we Indian. I knew Bob spent a good deal of time in the mountains and had done much tracking of his own for wild game, and as we

> As I cooked our evening meal Bob fed the horses and we settled down to talk over events of the next day and to plan our trip up to Ape Canyon. The black of the night settled around the camp and we began to hear coyotes on the ridge howl their lonesome wails to the sky. Bob had taken his faithful German Shepherd, Ace, along and we were amused at his expressions when he heard the coyotes.

An excerpt from Patterson's book *Do Abominable Snowmen of America Really Exist?* In this excerpt, Patterson and Gimlin travel to Mount St. Helens and Ape Canyon.

> When I returned from my latest pre-expedition, much to my surprise I received a phone call which related an amazing story of

When Roger and Bob returned home from Mount St. Helens, he received a phone call. I like to point this out because this is also told in Roger Patterson story on why he gone to Bluff Creek Ca.

As the story goes soon after Roger and Bob return from Mount St. Helens. Roger received a phone call from John Green talking about Bigfoot tracks they found in Blue Creek Mountains in California.

By carefully dissecting Patterson's book, we find in separate stories details that, when taken together, comprise the P/G Bluff Creek film story. The Bluff Creek storyline is laid out in the book!

Now keep in mind that Roger Patterson's book was published in fall 1966. And what is told in Roger Patterson and Bob Gimlin stories after October of 1967 fits the same stories that are told in Roger book one year earlier.

In Patterson's book, Roger states that he and Bob Gimlin traveled to Mount St. Helens in September. They also claim that when they got back, they got a call from John Green who was down in the Blue Creek Mountain area; Green said that he had just found fresh Bigfoot tracks.

How can Roger and Bob have gone to Mount St. Helens in September of 1967 when in fact (if true) Roger and Bob journeyed to Mount St. Helens in September that took place before 1966 and before Roger book was published in the fall of 1966.

Again I like to point out that when John Green and Rene Dahendin was in the Blue Creek Mountain area in California in September of 1967, Roger and Bob claimed they was at Mount St. Helens and there is when Roger was talking to Bob about Bigfoot. But in Roger Patterson book from 1966 tells the same story of Roger and Bob going to Mount St. Helens and Roger talking to Bob about Bigfoot.

In short, Patterson lays out the Bluff Creek storyline in a book published in 1966, a year before he and Gimlin went to Bluff Creek. The circumstances of why they traveled to Bluff Creek in 1967 matches the same circumstances as their trip to Mount St. Helens *two years earlier*—in 1965. The Bluff Creek storyline is foreshadowed in Patterson's book. A remarkable set of coincidences?

Last, we have to look at the time frame of the Patterson and Gimlin 1967 Bigfoot film story.

Time frame

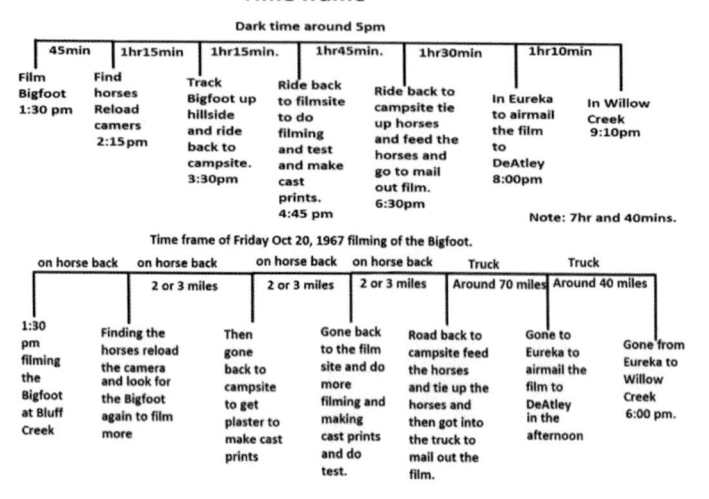

Dark time around 5pm

45min	1hr15min	1hr15min.	1hr45min.	1hr30min	1hr10min	
Film Bigfoot 1:30 pm	Find horses Reload camers 2:15pm	Track Bigfoot up hillside and ride back to campsite. 3:30pm	Ride back to filmsite to do filming and test and make cast prints. 4:45 pm	Ride back to campsite tie up horses and feed the horses and go to mail out film. 6:30pm	In Eureka to airmail the film to DeAtley 8:00pm	In Willow Creek 9:10pm

Note: 7hr and 40mins.

Time frame of Friday Oct 20, 1967 filming of the Bigfoot.

on horse back	on horse back	on horse back	on horse back	Truck	Truck	
	2 or 3 miles	2 or 3 miles	2 or 3 miles	Around 70 miles	Around 40 miles	
1:30 pm filming the Bigfoot at Bluff Creek	Finding the horses reload the camera and look for the Bigfoot again to film more	Then gone back to campsite to get plaster to make cast prints	Gone back to the film site and do more filming and making cast prints and do test.	Road back to campsite feed the horses and tie up the horses and then got into the truck to mail out the film.	Gone to Eureka to airmail the film to DeAtley in the afternoon	Gone from Eureka to Willow Creek 6:00 pm.

This time frame is based on what Patterson and Gimlin claimed to have done as they filmed the Bigfoot and after the filming was complete. Using the time frame explained in various sources, we see that it took Patterson 7 hours and 40 minutes to do everything the men claimed. But then again, keep in mind that it got dark around 5:00 PM at this time of year.

Chapter Three: Roger Patterson's Book.

Cover of Roger Patterson's book called *Do Abominable Snowmen of America Really Exist?*

Published in the fall of 1966

Roger Patterson's book was ostensibly based on his own experiences and on eyewitness accounts. In the book Roger presents some of the adventures he and his partner experienced as well as eyewitness Bigfoot sightings. Roger illustrated the stories in pen and ink.

Drawing made by Roger Patterson for his book.

Roger Patterson created all the drawings in the book. However, he found himself in hot water over some of the drawings he used in the book. Presented here is one Roger Patterson's drawings that got him into copyright infringement troubles.

"Both Were Surprised"

83

The drawing presented here was copied from an article written by Ivan Sanderson.

Other drawings in Roger's book were copied from other books and articles, which he claimed were his own.

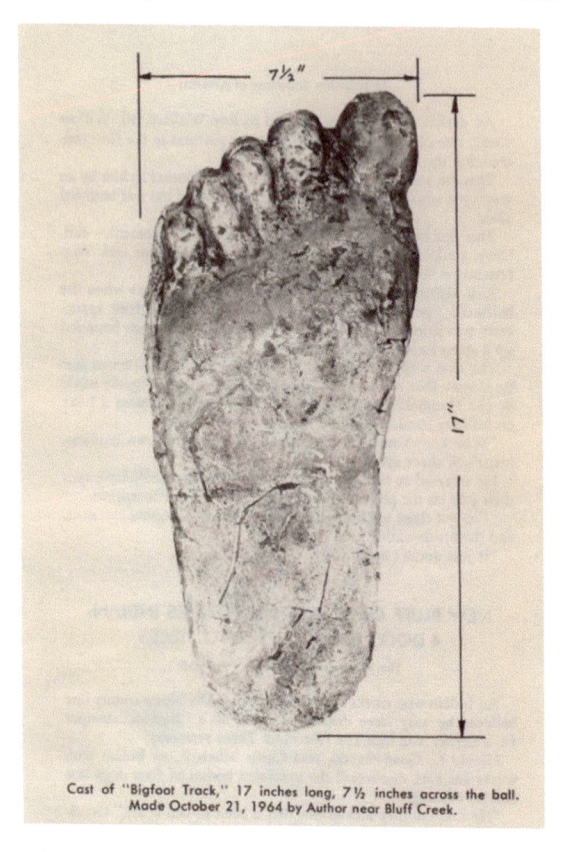

Cast of "Bigfoot Track," 17 inches long, 7½ inches across the ball. Made October 21, 1964 by Author near Bluff Creek.

Image from Roger's book of a Bigfoot cast he claimed he made.

84

Not only did Patterson copy other artists' drawings, he supposedly cast a Bigfoot print at Bluff Creek on October 21, 1964. However, if one studies the cast and compares its shape to the drawing of a Bigfoot print in his book, the two are remarkably the same. How did two supposedly different Bigfoots produce prints that matched perfectly?

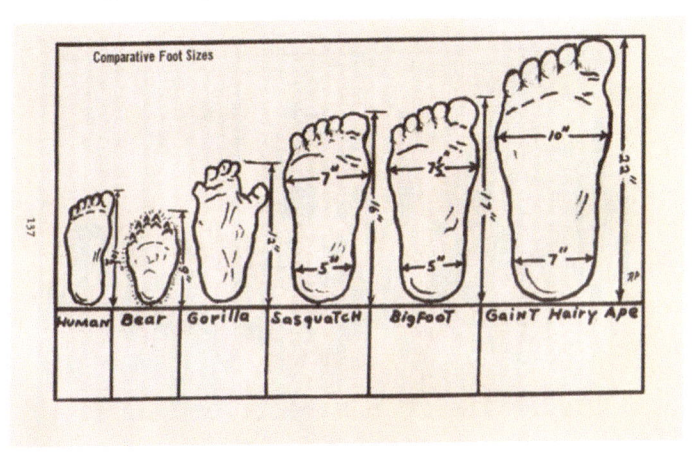

Drawings Roger Patterson created depicting the size of Bigfoot and humans, and bears and gorillas. The drawing above to the far right the Giant Hairy Ape is the same as the Bigfoot cast Roger Patterson made.

85

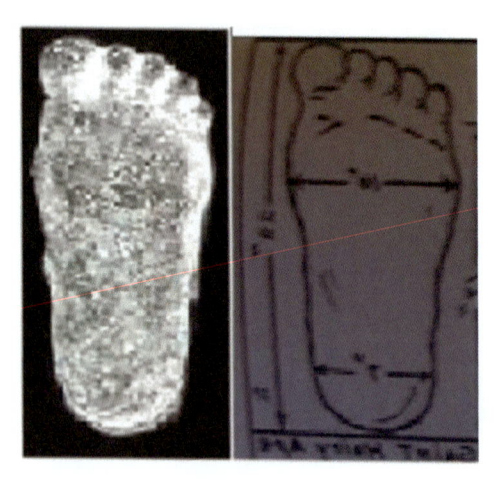

The cast print Roger Patterson made after he filmed the Bigfoot at Bluff Creek Ca. 1967. The drawing of a Sasquatch foot prints that Roger done and place in his book in 1966. As you see the drawing and the cast print are one in the same.

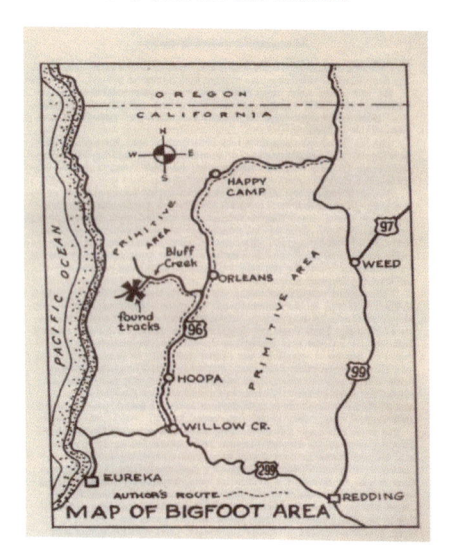

86

A map drawing by Roger Patterson.

When I looked over this map that is in Roger Patterson book from 1966 shows the same rout Roger took in 1967. Even the same location marked on this map is the same location were Roger filmed his Bigfoot (Bluff Creek).

A close scrutiny of Patterson's 1966 book uncovers numerous details that match his Bigfoot film experience that occurred a year later.

From Patterson book 1966

From Patterson film 1967

Notably, the drawing of a female Bigfoot in Roger Patterson's book matches the Bigfoot he filmed!

ASSIGNMENT AND BILL OF SALE

IN CONSIDERATION of the payment by the Grantee of $500.00 to ROGER PATTERSON, the Grantor, receipt of which payment is hereby acknowledged, the Grantor hereby sells, assigns, transfers and conveys to GLEN A. KOELLING all property rights, copyrights, and all other of the Grantor's property and interest in and to the book "Do Abominable Snowmen of America Really Exist?", of which book Roger Patterson is the author, and which book is published by The Franklin Press, Yakima, Washington, 1966, to have and to hold unto the Grantee, his heirs and assigns forever.

DATED at Yakima, Washington this 27 day of October, 1966.

Roge Patterson
GRANTOR.

STATE OF WASHINGTON } ss.
County of Yakima }

On this day personally appeared before me ROGER PATTERSON, to me known to be the individual described in and who executed the within and foregoing instrument, and acknowledged that he signed the same as his free and voluntary act and deed, for the uses and purposes therein mentioned.

GIVEN under my hand and official seal this 27 day of October, 1966.

NOTARY PUBLIC in and for the State of Washington, residing at Yakima.

Filed for Record OCT 27 1966
Request of G. A. KOELLING
EUGENE NAFF, County Auditor

With Roger Patterson not making any money on his book, he sold the copyright to Glen A. Koelling for the sum of $500 just weeks after the book was released.

When the second edition of Roger's book came out in 1968, published by Ron Olson, neither Mr. Koelling nor anyone in his family ever received one dime off of Roger's book although he still owned the copyright. He did not contest Olson's "ownership" in court.

Chapter Four: Documentary

Most of the public does not know it, but in 1967 Roger Patterson and some friends were filming a documentary called *Bigfoot-America's Abominable Snowman*.

The stars, all from Yakima, who played in Roger Patterson's documentary (left to right): Roger Patterson, John Ballard, Jerry Merritt, Howard Heironimus, Bob Gimlin, and Bob Heironimus.

The documentary storyline is that a group of men, with the help of a Native American played by Bob Gimlin, using tracking dogs, embarked on a hunt for Bigfoot. The cowboy hunters mostly sit around a campfire telling stories. Bob Gimlin, who it is claimed has a smidgeon of Apache blood, wore a wig with Indian tresses.

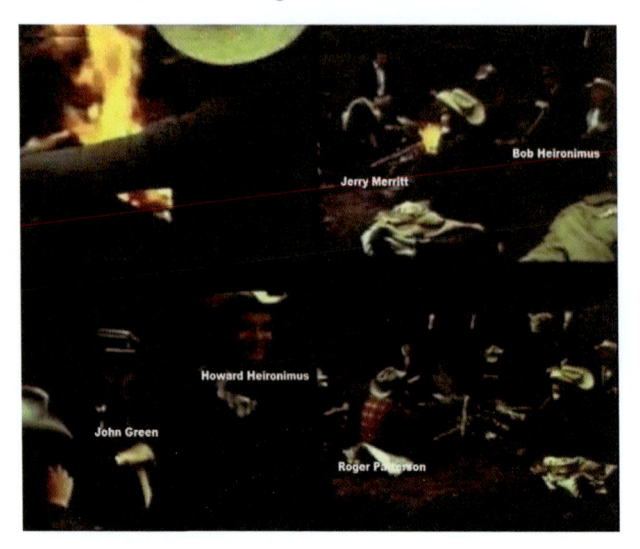

Frames from the documentary.

90

Very few people have viewed this documentary in its totality. However, a few pieces of it exist, for example, footage of the cowboy Bigfoot hunters sitting around a campfire telling stories. Interestingly, one of the pieces shows two other men, and they weren't from Yakima: John Green and Rene Dahendin, famed Canadian Bigfoot investigators.

Few people also know that the P/G film, that is, the short sequence of the Bluff Creek Bigfoot walking, was stitched together with some of the Yakima cowboy Bigfoot hunter's footage into a documentary. Then, in 1968, a second documentary was made, and the cowboy footage was removed.

Bob Heironimus

Roger Patterson

Jerry Merritt

In the first documentary, one scene shows two men riding down a steep hillside; one of them has a rope attached to a packhorse. The narrator of the documentary states that the two men were Roger Patterson and Bob Gimlin. However, close examination of the scene reveals that two men were, in fact, Jerry Merritt and Bob Heironimus.

Roger Patterson

More frames from Roger Patterson Documentary film.

In another documentary sequence, we see Roger Patterson squatting down and making cast prints and then standing and holding them. When the film was remade into the second documentary, the claim was made that, indeed, Patterson made the cast prints—but that the cast prints he is holding were the casts of the Bigfoot that he had filmed at Bluff Creek! The fact is, based on a study of the environment and vegetation, the film snippet of Patterson casting and holding the prints was shot somewhere other than Bluff Creek. The cast prints Roger is holding are fakes that he made as a prop to be used in the documentary!

Roger Patterson and Rene Dahendin with horses in Volkswagen vans.

In Patterson's first documentary that he was working on with John Green and Rene Dahinden, the same Volkswagen vans shown in the photo provided here were

93

altered: the name on the top of the van was changed to Bigfoot 67 Expedition.

In the beginning of 1967, Roger Patterson and his friends produced a lot of footage to be used in the first documentary. However, when questioned later about the documentary, not one of them would answer questions. All that Patterson and Gimlin wanted to talk about was the amazing Bigfoot they filmed as it leisurely walked across the Bluff Creek sand bed in October 1967.

In my investigations, I found out that from January to the first part of May in 1967, Roger was filming scenes of his Bigfoot "expedition" at different locations. Soon after the filming was completed, he borrowed money from some friends to enable him to travel to Los Angeles, California, to sell his footage.

Contract for a loan.

A fact that is always overlooked by Patterson and Gimlin supporters is that Patterson borrowed the sum of $700 from a local woman, Vilma Radford, to take the film to Los Angeles. In a signed contract, he promised Radford that he would pay her back the sum of $850 plus 5% in royalties from sales of the film. Many P/G film proponents state that Roger borrowed money from Radford merely to pay for a camera and to film the documentary. But as the contract reads, Patterson promised to repay her by June 10, 1967. This time frame gives the total time of 15 days to take the film to Los Angeles and sell the film. If the loan was only to rent the camera and make the film, fifteen days is not enough time to shoot all the needed footage, have it developed, prepare it, make contacts in Hollywood, travel to Los Angeles, and find a producer to buy his documentary. But Patterson had already shot his Bigfoot "expedition" scenes early in 1967, from January to May! Therefore, he lied to Radford.

To explore more regarding Vilma Radford, the contract, and Patterson's false promises, refer to Greg Long's book *The Making of Bigfoot*.

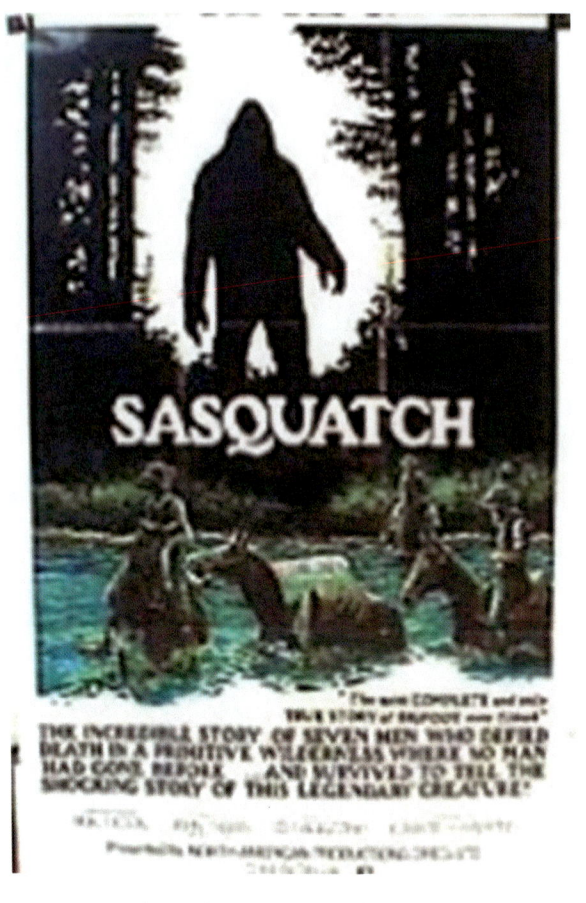

Sasquatch - The Legend of Bigfoot poster.

The reason why no one talks about Roger Patterson's early documentary projects is that in 1974, Ron Olson of the film production company American National Enterprises (ANE), remade Roger Patterson's documentary.

Sasquatch - The Legend of Bigfoot was filmed in 1974 but not released until March 9, 1977, 10 years after Roger Patterson filmed his Bigfoot.

The reason Ron Olson waited as long as he did was to "borrow" Patterson's story, hoping no one would notice that he purloined Patterson's idea. Ron Olson claimed it was his own story to avoid paying royalties to Roger Patterson's family.

The cast and crew who worked on Ron Olson's film, *Sasquatch – The Legend of Bigfoot.*

Side-by-side frames from Patterson's film and Ron Olson's film.

In Patterson's documentary, Bob Gimlin is wearing an Indian wig. Gimlin's character would be the Native American tracker with tracking dogs. The man on the right in Ron Olson's film is Joel Morello who played the Native American tracker Techka Blackhawk.

When I asked John Green to comment on the fact that Ron Olson used Roger Patterson's storyline, he replied as follows:

John Green: I was the person retained by American National when they made their documentary.
I organized the computer survey that they financed, and I took their crew around to get the interviews etc. that the documentary contained. They were hoping with the computer to determine a location where they could get their own sasquatch movie, and only turned to using Roger's movie when the computer attempt proved to be useless.

So, Green admits that Olson did use Patterson's story. When John Green told me that he (John Green) worked on Olson's movie, I uncovered an interesting item that avid P/G Bigfoot film fans overlooked.

Pair of fake Bigfoot shoes made by John Green.

Track from Ron Olson documentary from 1974

John Green and Rene Dehindend tracking dog film from 1967 Bluff Creek

Note:

Olson's film was shot in 1974, but it was not released until 1977. From here on, I will refer to the date Olson filmed his movie, 1974, and not the 1977 release date.

The tracks that we see in John Green tracking dog film from 1967 appears in Olson's 1974 film. With this new evidence, a series of questions demand answers.

100

John Green's pair of Bigfoot shoes from his film appear in Olson's film. The films were shot seven years apart, and at different locations.

Also in Ron Olson film from 1974 we see the same Bigfoot track from which Roger Patterson made a cast print in 1967.

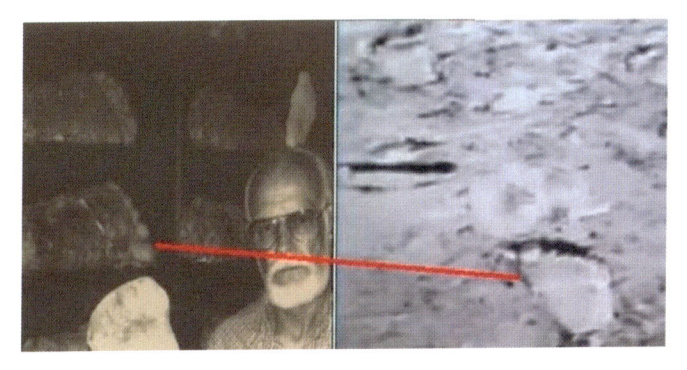

Bigfoot tracks made by Bob Titmus, a Northern California Bigfoot investigator, can also be seen in Ron Olson film from 1974.

Odd. The same Bigfoot tracks keep showing up wherever John Green shows up. Were the tracks Green discovered in 1967 at Bluff Creek real or fake?

John Green was a good friend of Roger Patterson and Ron Olson. He was also good friends with Bob Titmus. The tracking dog film Bigfoot prints and Roger Patterson's Bigfoot prints and even Bob Titmus's Bigfoot prints all appear in Ron Olson's film.

Another curiosity is the Bigfoot suit (or costume). It turns out that Ron Olson used a Bigfoot suit that Mr. Phillip Morris sold to Roger Patterson in the summer of 1967 (see Greg Long's *The Making of Bigfoot*). Apparently, the suit was kept by Al DeAtley, Roger Patterson's brother-in-law. DeAtley knew both John Green and Ron Olson; he let them use the suit.

More on this fascinating finding as we go along.

Chapter Five: Copyrights

Who owns the copyrights to the P/G film?

For many years, researchers have been trying to ascertain who really owns the copyright to the P/G film. In the beginning there was only one person who owned the copyright: Roger Patterson.

However, after Roger passed away, the copyrights were turned over to Roger's widow, Mrs. Patterson (Patricia Patterson). However, in 1984 Bob Gimlin took her to court, which revised the copyright to the film. The story goes that Robert Gimlin soon after securing his copyright to the film, sold his rights over to Rene Dahinden for the sum of $10 (some say it was the price of a cup of coffee).

When I discussed the copyright issue with John Green in 2010, I asked him who owns the copyright to the film and who possesses the original film.

John Green: I don't have the facts myself but I am told that the original film was left in storage with the company that made the first documentary. Roger, of course, died. That company later folded and the film passed into possession of another company, which also went bankrupt. A third company now has the film, but ownership is in dispute.

If Mrs. Patterson owns the copyright to the film, why did John Green tell me the ownership is in dispute?

One way to settle the dispute is to search the files of the United States Copyright Office in the Library of Congress.

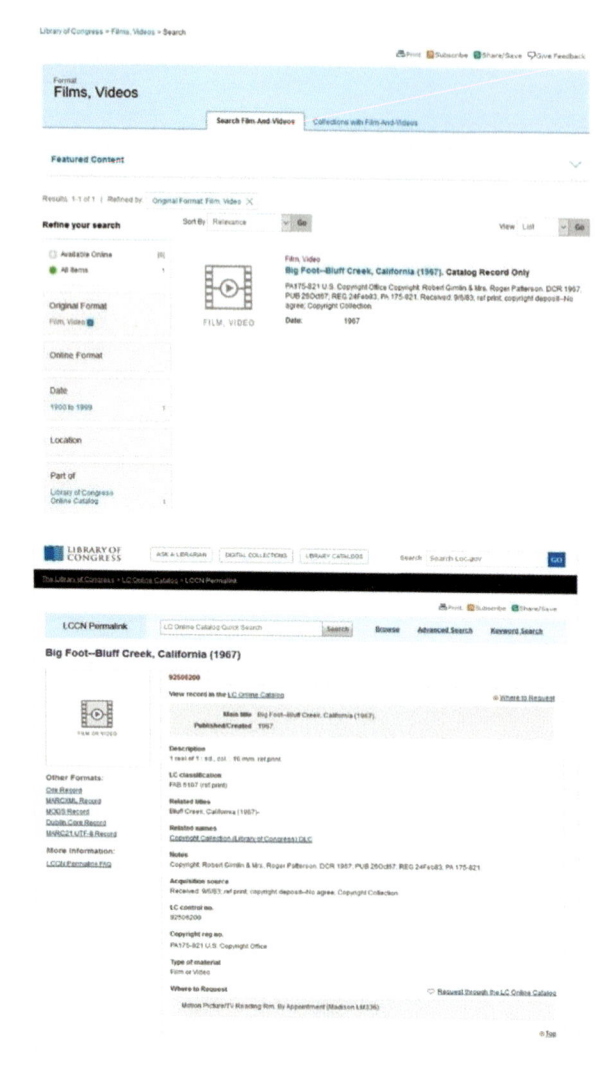

Website:

https://catalog.loc.gov/vwebv/search?searchCode=STNO
&searchArg=92506200&searchType=1&recCount=10

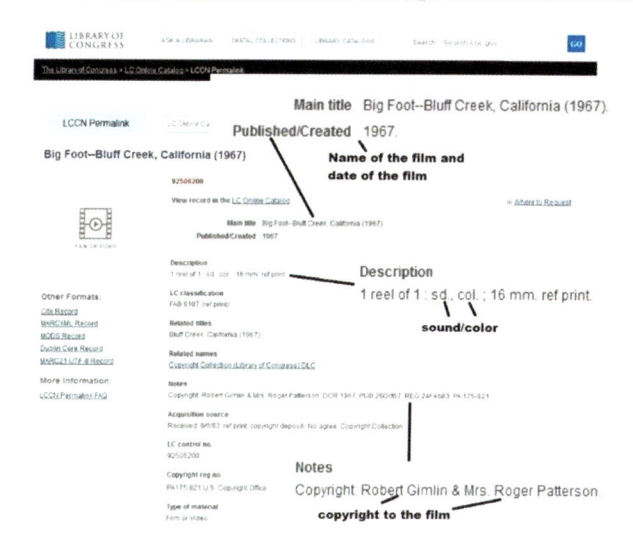

[Screenshot of Library of Congress catalog record with annotations pointing to:]
- Name of the film and date of the film: "Big Foot--Bluff Creek, California (1967)"
- Description: "1 reel of 1 : sd., col. ; 16 mm. ref print." — sound/color
- Notes: "Copyright: Robert Gimlin & Mrs. Roger Patterson" — copyright to the film

Information in the Library of Congress indicates that the owners of the film are Robert Gimlin and Patricia Patterson. Importantly, however, the copyright to the film in question is entitled *Bigfoot - Bluff Creek, California 1967*.

However, the film that researchers have long been studying, and the copy of the film that Patricia Patterson possesses, are a *different* film.

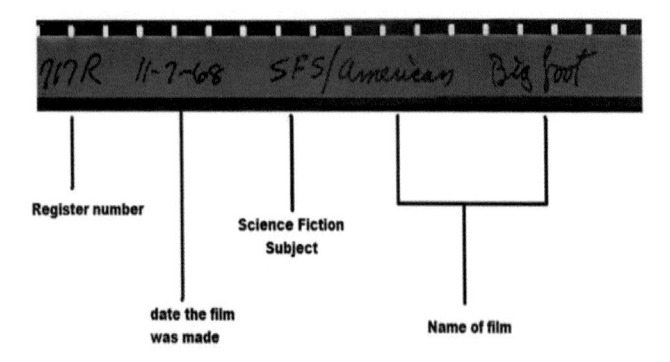

- Register number
- date the film was made
- Science Fiction Subject
- Name of film

The very end of the Patterson and Gimlin Bigfoot film

The very end of the P/G film.

As the P/G Bigfoot film reveals, the footage Patterson shot at Bluff Creek is marked as *American Bigfoot*; the date of the film is 1968.

When Roger Patterson turned over the original film to Ron Olson in 1968, Olson remade the film for Roger and after he (Ron Olson) remade the film they never got the film copyrighted under the new name American Bigfoot.

This is why John Green said that the ownership of the film was in dispute because the original film called Bluff Creek Bigfoot 1967 was copyrighted, but when it was remade in 1968 by Ron Olson of ANE and they changed the name of the film to American Bigfoot 1968 they never had the copyright transfer over to the new film.

This is why today there is no one that has the copyright to the film called American Bigfoot 1968. And the film that Mrs. Patterson and John Green has in their possession is the film called American Bigfoot 1968. The film that has copyright on is Bluff Creek Bigfoot 1967 and that film is no long existing.

In short, there are two films, and only one of the films is copyrighted. That film (original P/G film) was cut up and placed into a remade film that no one took the time to copyright.

To add to the confusion, some believe that Roger Patterson owns the rights to the whole film 3min film called Bluff Creek Bigfoot 1967, but John Green and Rene Dahinden own the copyrights for Canada. They paid the sum of $1500 to own the rights. But they received only thirty seconds of the film that shows the second part of the Bigfoot walking. Why weren't they given the first 30 seconds? Was something hidden from them?

Chapter Six: Filming Location

Controversy still rages nearly 50 years later regarding the filming location of the P/G Bluff Creek Bigfoot. If the location is in dispute, did Patterson and Gimlin deceive the public, spinning a tale to fit their story? Controversy also swirls around the tracking dog film.

As I discovered, self-proclaimed Bigfoot researchers claim to have found the true filming location, but there is no real evidence to back it.

Until now.

Photo taken by Rene Dahinden.

The image above shows the Patterson and Gimlin film site. The image is from a film taken by Rene Dahinden in the 1970s. Other Bigfoot researchers took images of the filming site, but this is the only image that presents an aerial view.

When I was searching for the film site, I reviewed many files and maps produced over the years that claim to show the actual filming site. However, the documentation places the filming site at locations all up and down Bluff Creek. When asked about the actual filming site, Bob Gimlin and John Green answered that they had forgotten the true location with the passing of time.

To determine if the local environment was conducive to allow the passage of men on horseback and a Bigfoot to cross a clearing such as described by Patterson, it is necessary to identify the true film site.

After months of looking on Google Earth, I finally uncovered the true location of the Patterson and Gimlin Bigfoot film site.

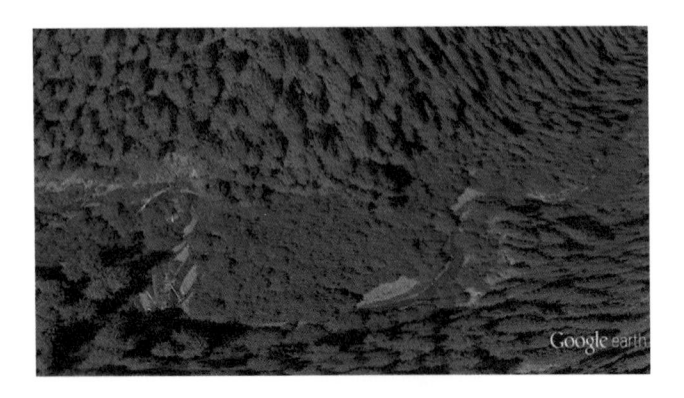

Image from Google earth

This image above is the true location of the film site where Roger Patterson and Bob Gimlin filmed the walking Bigfoot.

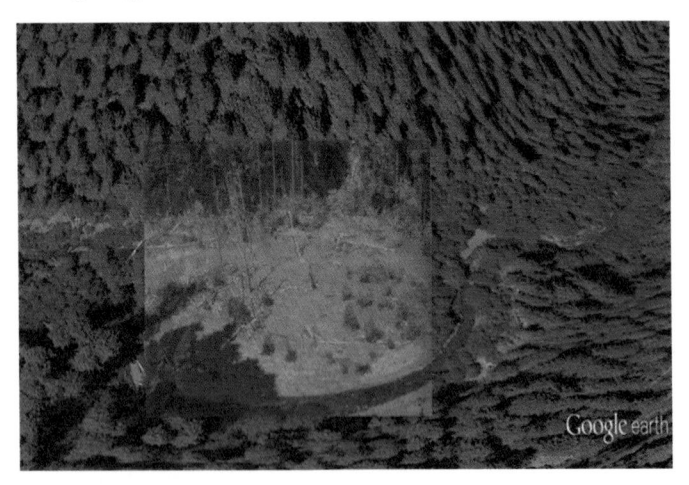

Match.

110

The film site measurements.
295.15ft by 433.22ft.
Or
105.15 yards by 147.94 yards.

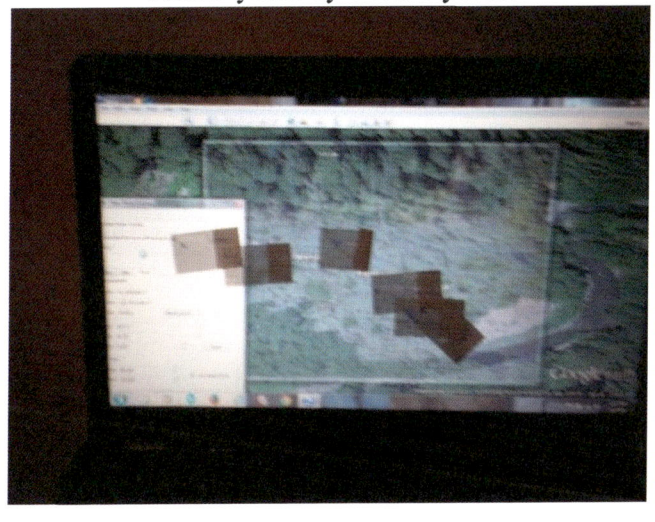

Mapping out the rout the Bigfoot walking in the P/G Bigfoot film.

After pinpointing the Bigfoot route, I found the locations where Roger started to film and when the Bigfoot turned and looked back.

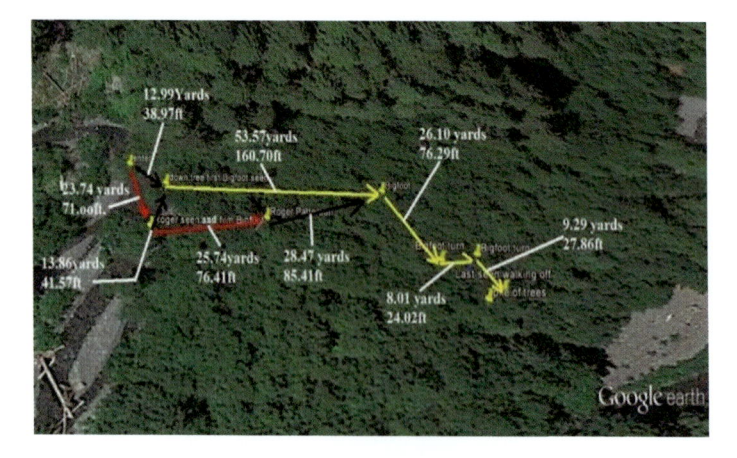

By finding the filming site and by pinpointing the route the Bigfoot took, I was able to make proper measurements the rout the Bigfoot took and the distance between Roger Patterson and the Bigfoot.

Measurements revealed that Roger Patterson was not as far back from the Bigfoot as he claimed when he started to film the Bigfoot and as he ran up on the Bigfoot while continuing to film. Plus, we now can see that the Bigfoot route was not as long as claimed over the years.

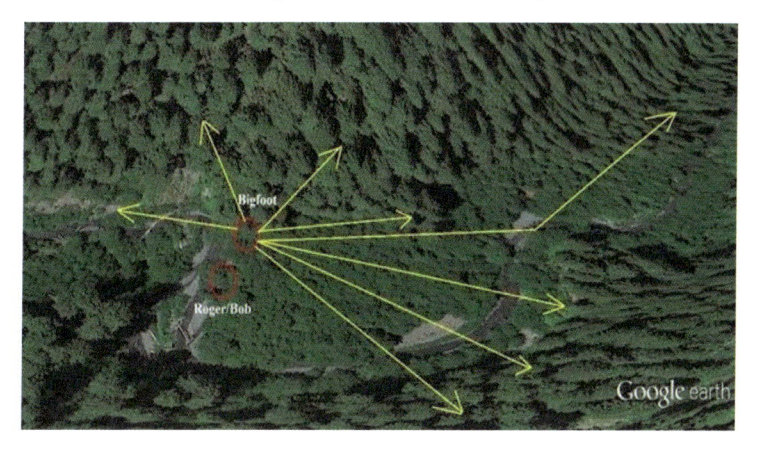

When trying to line up the key points of the story with the layout of the film site, things go awry.

The conventional story claims that Patterson ran out of film, and that when the Bigfoot vanished from view, the Bigfoot ran off and up a hillside. (Of course, why did the Bigfoot merely walk in front of Patterson and then later run off? Shouldn't the reverse happen if a human was rushing the Bigfoot with a camera in hand?)

When viewing the film site, we see that the Bigfoot had at its disposal a variety of different exits it could have taken to escape the threat of two humans and their horses. If the Bigfoot would have run away via one of these closer exits, Patterson would have failed to take even one second of film.

When I point this out to other researchers, they always come up with an excuse, such as, "Well, the hillside was too steep for the creature to exit that way."

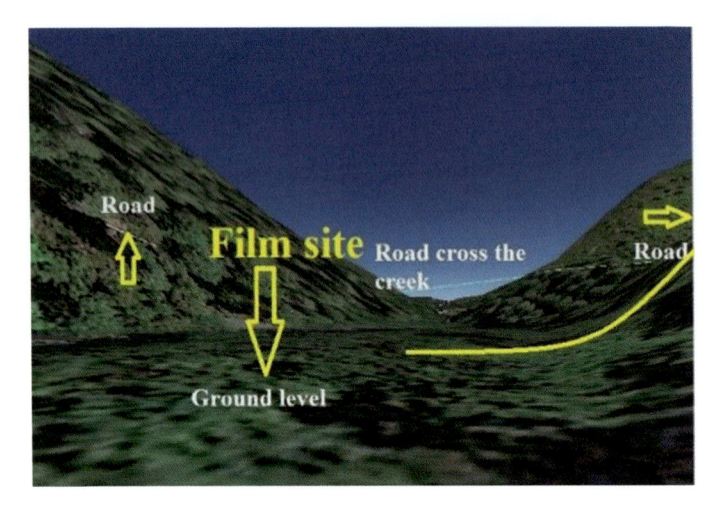

However, as Bob Gimlin told it, the Bigfoot ran up a hillside and ran down the road at the top of the hill. From the view included here, we can see both roads (one road to the right on the image is the road Bob Gimlin was talking about the Bigfoot travel down.). The road to the left is closer to the strolling Bigfoot than the road the creature ran down as Bob Gimlin and Roger Patterson stated.

As we see, the creature could also have run straight into the forest to escape Roger and Bob.

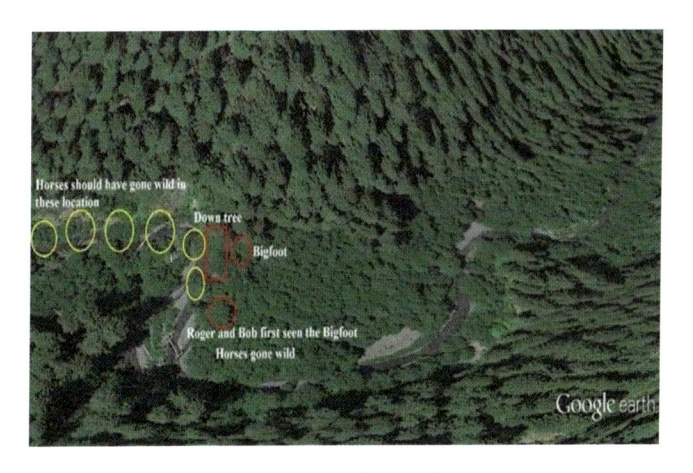

Another glaring oddity in the P/G film story is the "horses went wild" incident.

I've pointed this out before, but why did the horses only buck when they came right upon the creature? From my experience, horses have a sixth sense that alerts them to something out of place in the environment; this includes sounds and smells. Not until Patterson and Gimlin made a turn around the fallen tree did the horses buck.

When I was probing into the exact location of Patterson and Gimlin's film site, I pinpointed the locations where John Green and Rene Dahinden filmed the tracking dog film, the film of Jim McClarin walking the path of the Bigfoot and the location where Rene Dahdein shot his film of the P/G film site.

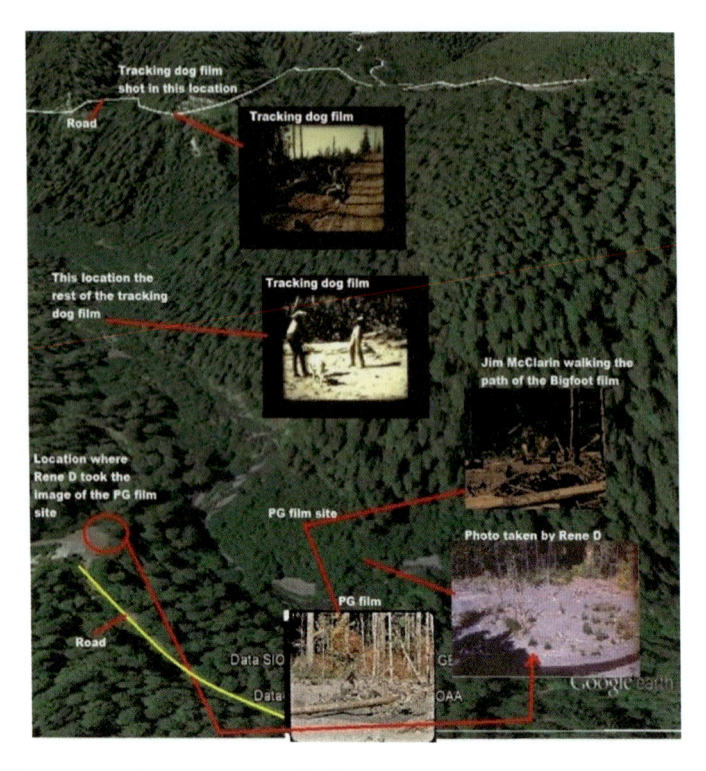

From the view presented above we see two roads sandwiching the PG Bigfoot film site between them. By examining the surroundings and the tracking dog film, it appears that all three of these films were shot in an area close to the same locations, but far from one another.

116

Chapter Seven: Bigfoot Suit

In almost half a century, a lot of claims have been made regarding the Bigfoot itself in the film. Is the Bigfoot a real uncatalogued animal or hominid, or just a man in a costume? Rumor has it that some people in the movie industry made the suit for Roger Patterson. However, there is only one story that has such veracity that it casts all the other stories into the shadows. Some people say that no one on earth can make a suit that looks like the one—if a suit—in the P/G film.

However, there is one man who says that he could make such a suit: Mr. Phillip Morris.

Before numerous audiences, he has stated that he sold to Roger Patterson a gorilla suit and that he told Patterson to make the suit look "real." He claimed to have sold Roger Patterson a brownish- red gorilla suit.

John Green claimed the creature in the original film was just plain black.

To answer the question as to who made the suit used in the P/G film, we have to look at what the creature looks like on the film itself. Is the creature a man in a suit or an unidentified man-like creature?

Frame 352 of the P/G film.

When we look closely at the creature in blow-ups we see details not heretofore seen.

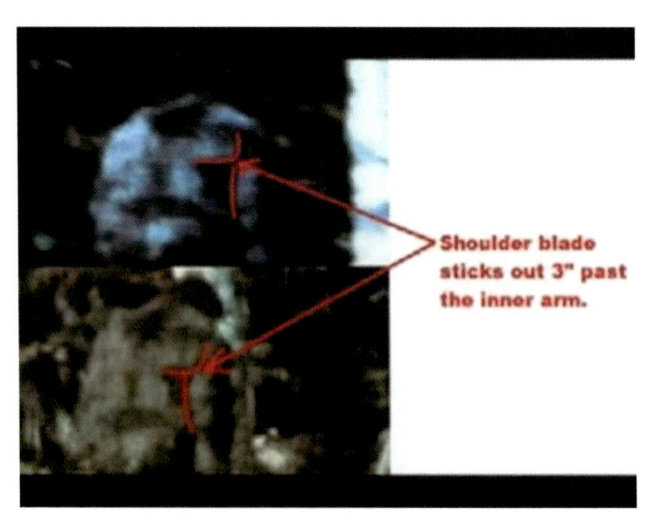

Shoulder blade sticks out 3" past the inner arm.

118

Shoulder blade goes past the inner arm 3in

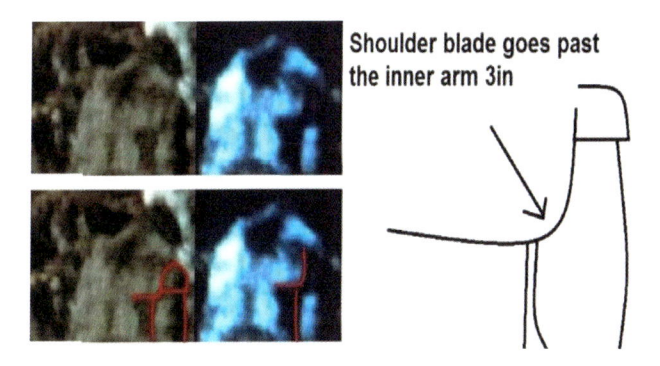

In the close-up of the back of the creature, we see that the shoulder blade on the creature sticks out past the inner arm.

If the shoulder blade extends outward as far as the film reveals, it would make it impossible for the creature's arm to come back into position. As the arm moves backward, the shoulder blade pushes forward. The close-up shows the form of an *artificial shoulder pad*.

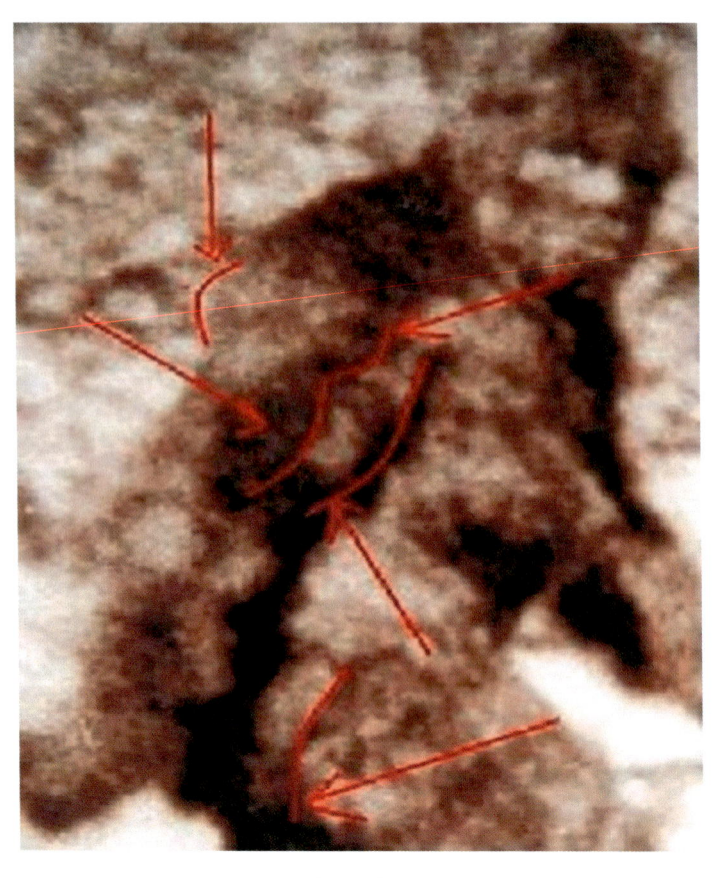

Side view.

In another sequence as the creature walks, we see that when the arm swings backward, the upper muscle in the arm folds together to form a *smaller arm* on the inside of the fur.

Also, the outline of a *shoulder pad* can be seen as well as a *seam* that separates the torso from the leg.

120

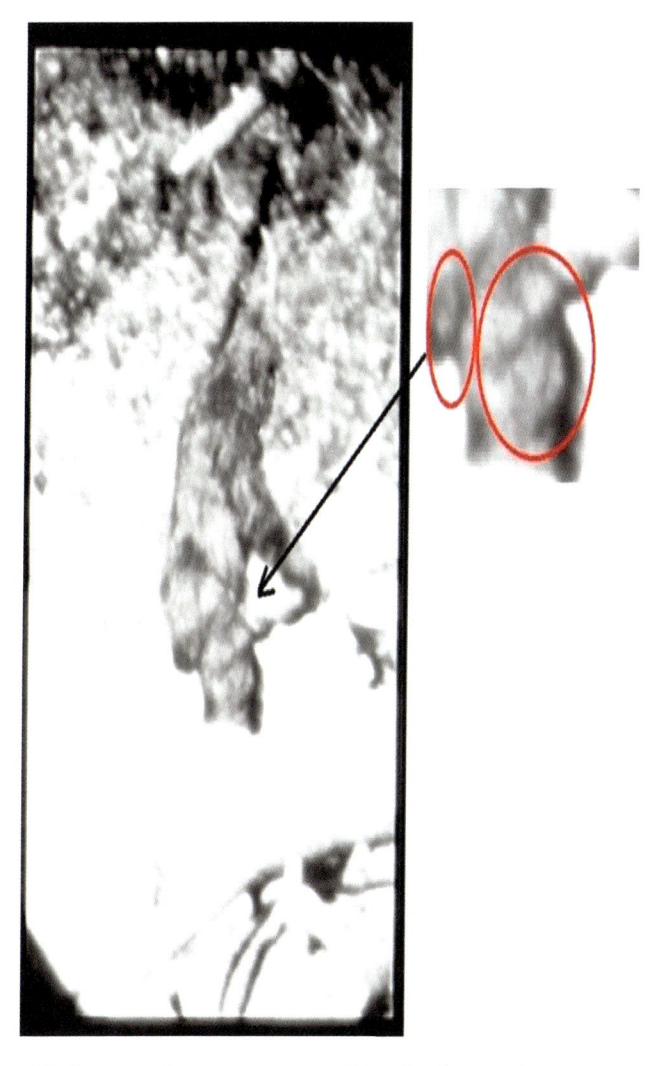

In addition, as the creature *walks*, the buttocks appear to be more stationary, and the fur on the leg bunches up like a person's *pants* would when he walks.

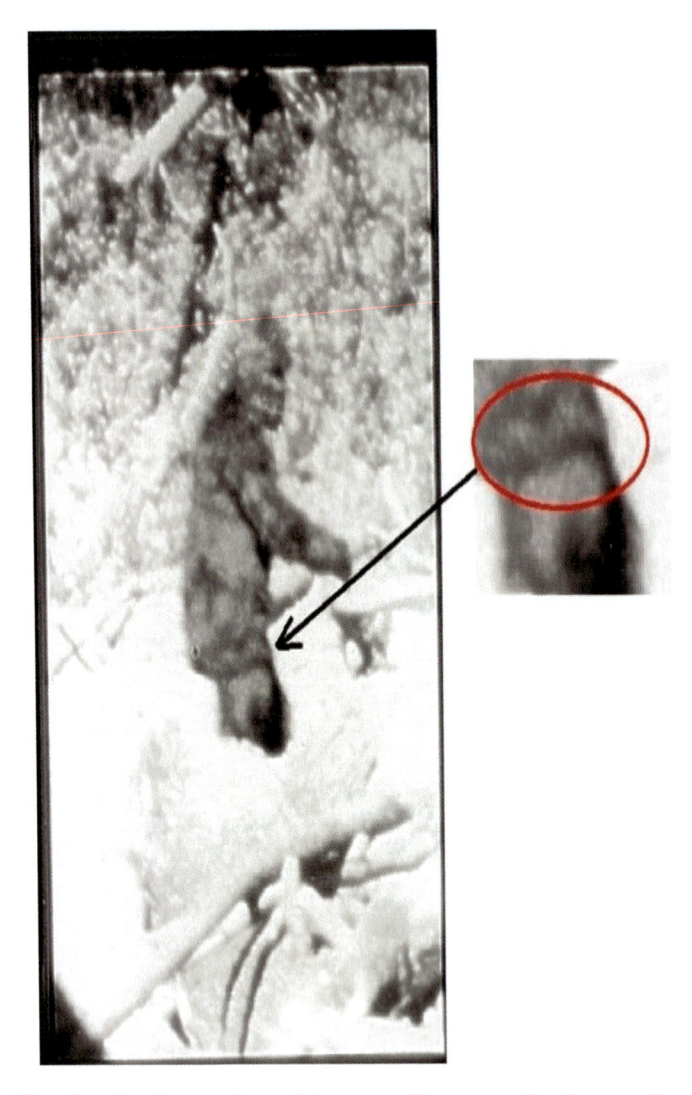

The leg fur keeps bunching up all across the leg as the Bigfoot walks.

122

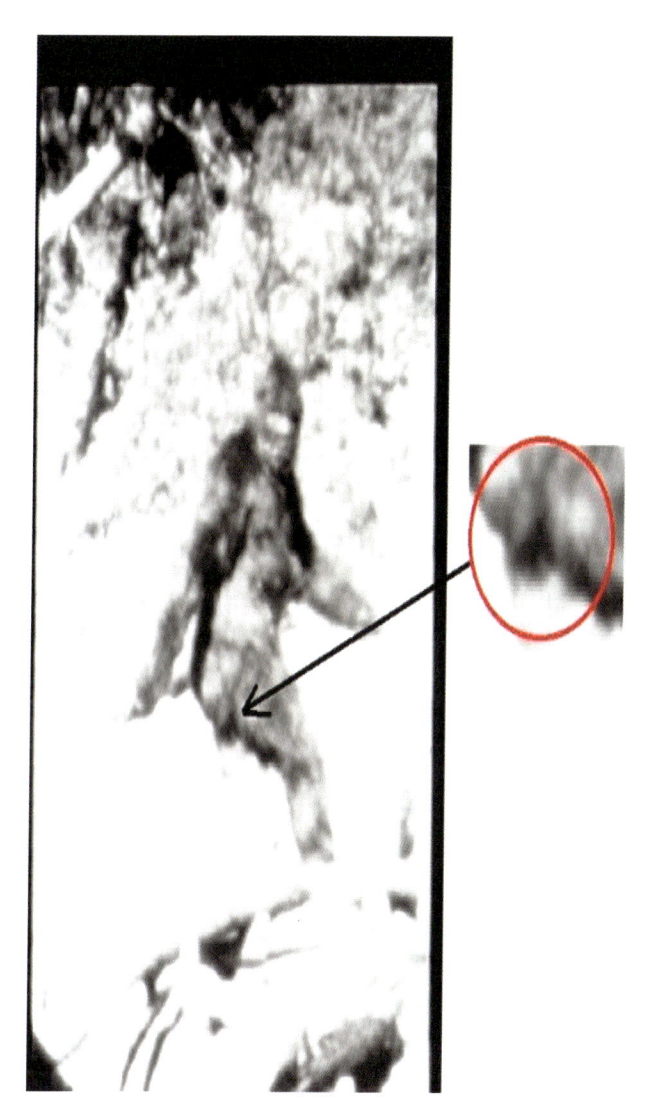

Then, further on in the walking sequence, some fur comes *untucked and hangs down* through the rest of the film.

Top of strap

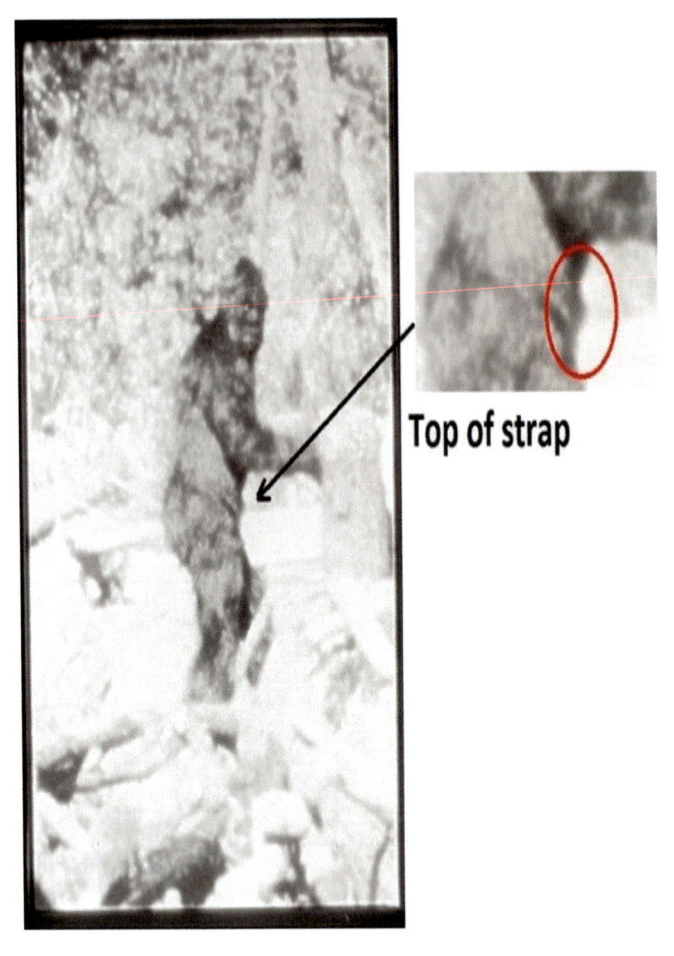

As the creature makes the turn to look back, a *strap* can be seen at the lower part of the pelvic area.

If these suspicious features were the only details we could consider to determine a hoax, we might discount these curiosities as mere artifacts or tricks of the eye. But there is more we can examine.

In the film the creature's hands open up as the arm swings back. Here is a close-up of the left hand.

By darkening the frame showing the left hand, the outline of the fingers can be seen.

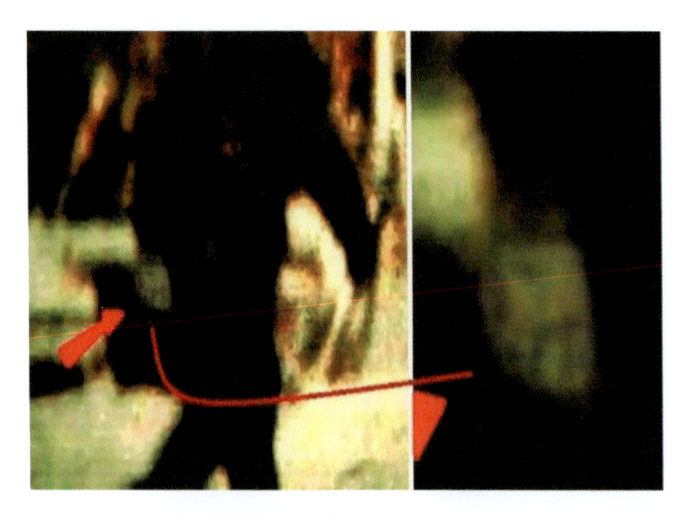

Darken the frame just a little more, and we now see for the first time the left hand of the creature.

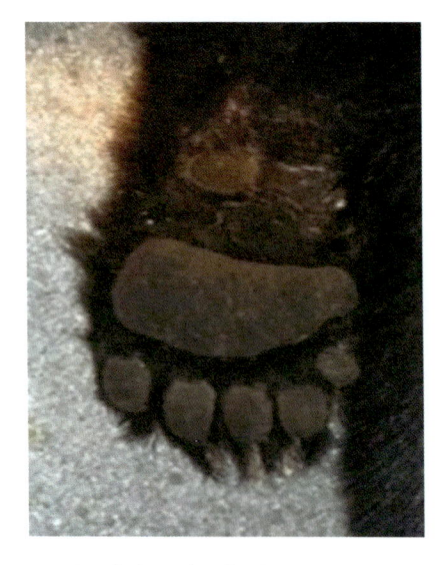

Left hand of a bear paw.

Close scrutiny tells us the type of creature this is: a bear, or at least a portion of the creature appears to be from a bear.

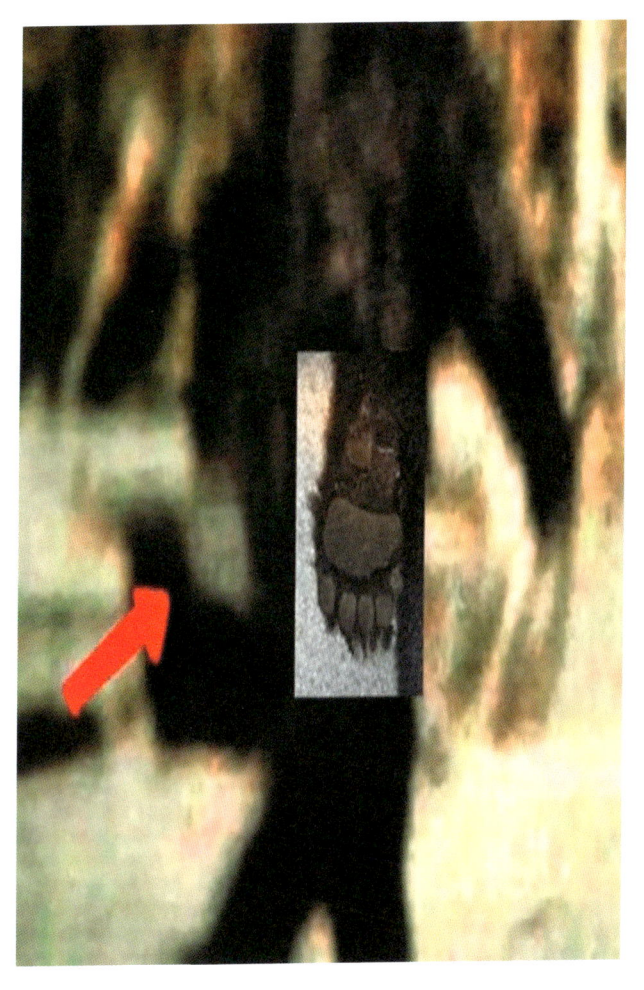

The left hand on the creature is a bear paw.

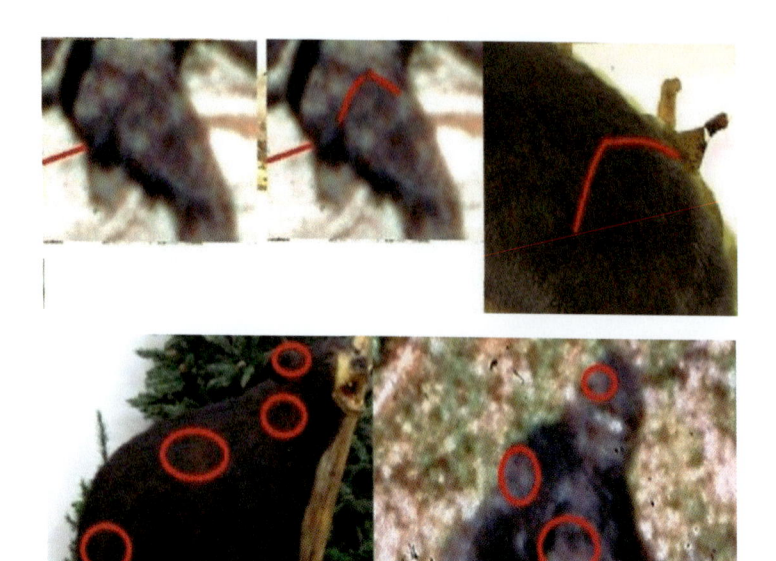

Because I suspected that the left hand of the creature is a bear paw, I studied bear hides and compared the fur on the creature to bear fur. When viewing images of stuffed bears, I also found the same type of seam that runs between the torso and the leg on the creature.

Further examination convinced me that the type of beast used to make the Bigfoot suit was a bear hide.

Now, we consider the feet on the P/G creature.

128

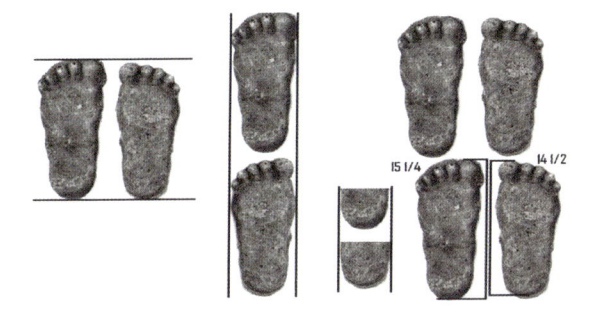

Cast prints Roger Patterson made.

The two prints Patterson made measure 15.25 inches long (one foot) and the other foot is 14.5 inches long.

Roger Patterson holds alleged cast prints he made from the creature he filmed.

Roger Patterson claimed that the cast prints he was holding were the cast prints of the creature he filmed at Bluff Creek.

With this information in hand, I lined up the image of the cast prints with the feet on the creature in the film.

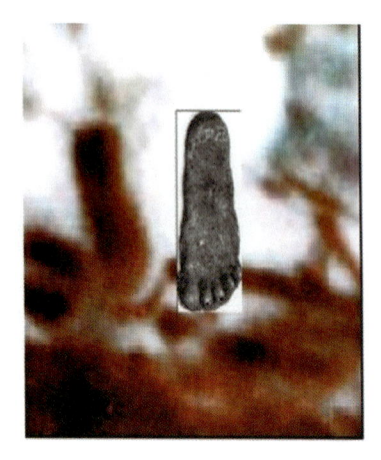

Negative of the feet on the creature from the film and the cast prints made by Roger Patterson.

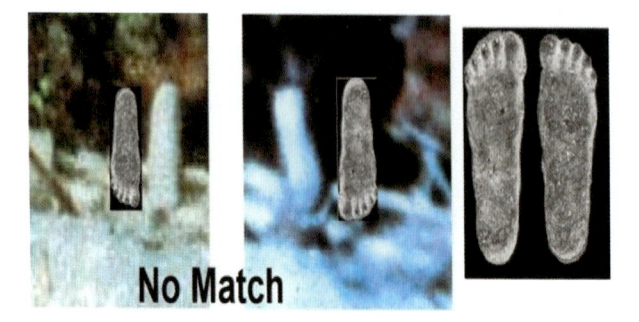

No Match

As one can see, the cast prints Patterson made do not match the feet of the Bigfoot in the film.

130

If they do not match, what type of feet does the creature possess? (And it appears Patterson lied.)

When I discovered that the film itself (P/G film) was created had been edited. I decided to clear up the area of the feet in an attempt to identify the feet as either manmade, a known mammal, or a creature unknown to man.

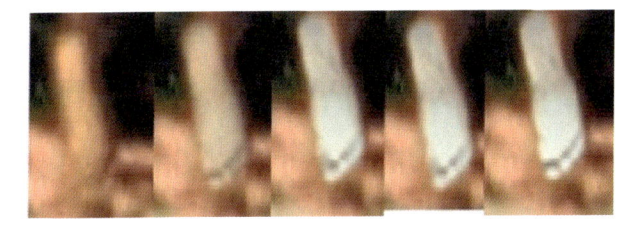

Close up of the right foot of the creature in the P/G film.

Knowing that the film was edited and that color and lighting had improved its quality, I found a method to clear up the feet. By outlining the foot area and adding more light and sharpening the feet, we now see a clear image of the feet on Roger Patterson's Bigfoot.

With a clear image of the feet in hand, I compared the right foot of Roger Patterson's Bigfoot to artificial Bigfoot shoes made by Ray Wallace. They matched! The same size and shape! (Wallace confessed to his family in for years that he had hoaxed Bigfoot tracks at Bluff Creek in 1958, which John Green declared to be authentic.)

After I clearing up the right foot of Patterson's Bigfoot, I did the same with the left foot of the Bigfoot.

I compared the image of the left foot to the left Bigfoot shoe made by Ray Wallace. Wallace's foot was the same shape and size as the left foot of Roger's Bigfoot.

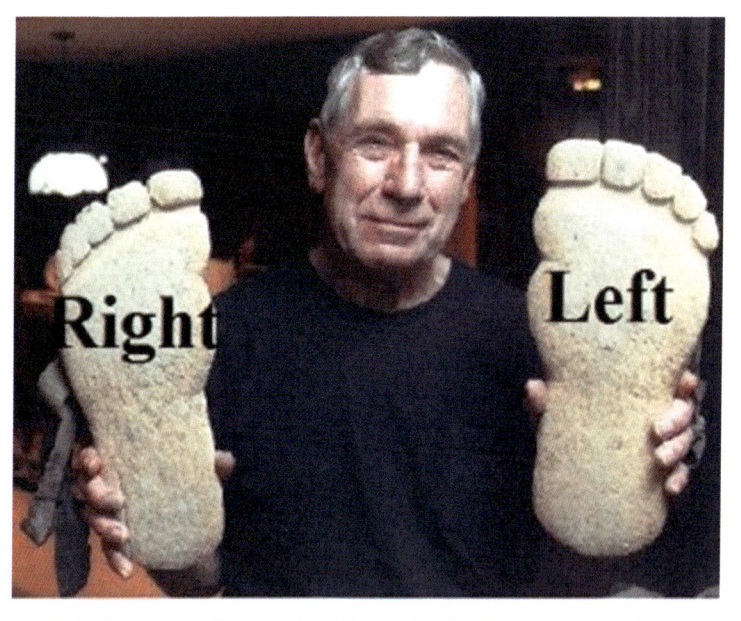

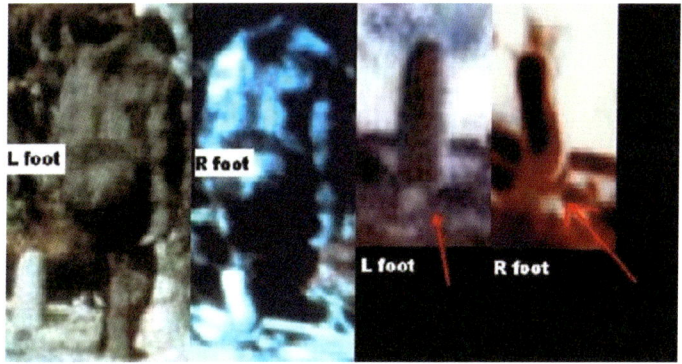

This finding would explain why Roger Patterson's Bigfoot feet did not match: the right foot is longer than the left foot, and the left foot is wider than the right foot.

Amazingly, Wallace's left foot is wider than the right foot and the right foot is longer than the left foot (see image).

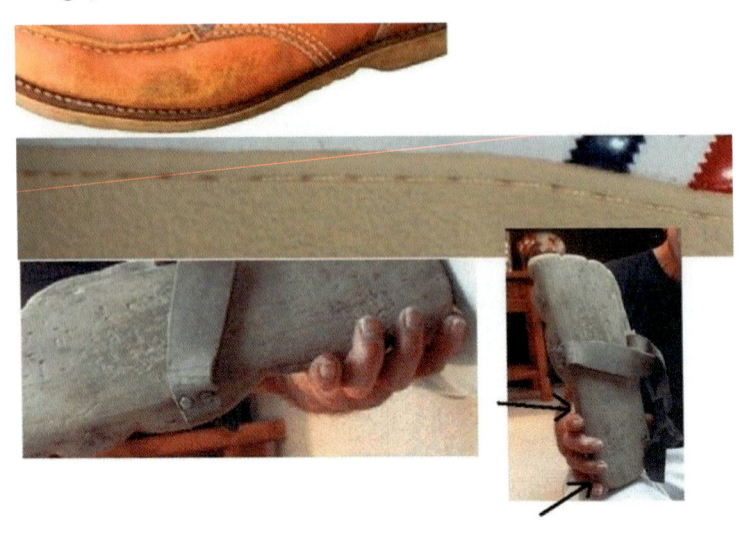

When viewing other images of a pair of Ray Wallace's Bigfoot shoes, we find that this one pair is the same shape and size as the feet on Roger Patterson's Bigfoot. On other images I found evidence that the sides of these same shoes have staple marks, which indicates that these Bigfoot shoes were attached to a suit at one time.

Simply put, Ray Wallace's Bigfoot shoes not only match the feet on Roger Patterson's Bigfoot, but the marks on the sides of these shoes show that they were attached to a suit.

Image of Bob Titmus.

More evidence exists that the Bigfoot in the P/G film is merely a man in a humanly constructed costume. Bob Titmus was a very good friend of Roger Patterson and John Green. Titmus's line of work was taxidermy. He owned and operated his own taxidermy shop 147 miles from where Patterson filmed his Bigfoot. Because Bob Titmus owned his own taxidermy shop and was practiced in taxidermy, he could very easily gain access to a bear hide. It would also make it easy for him to make the Bigfoot in the film seem more real than a run-of-the-mill costume maker.

Arm extensions.

Some researchers believe the arms on Roger Patterson's Bigfoot are longer than a normal man's arms. Phillip Morris, the world-renown costume maker, stated that Roger asked him in a phone conversation about arm extensions.

However, if the Bigfoot in the film is carefully studied, it seems that the Bigfoot's arms are the same length as a normal man's arms.

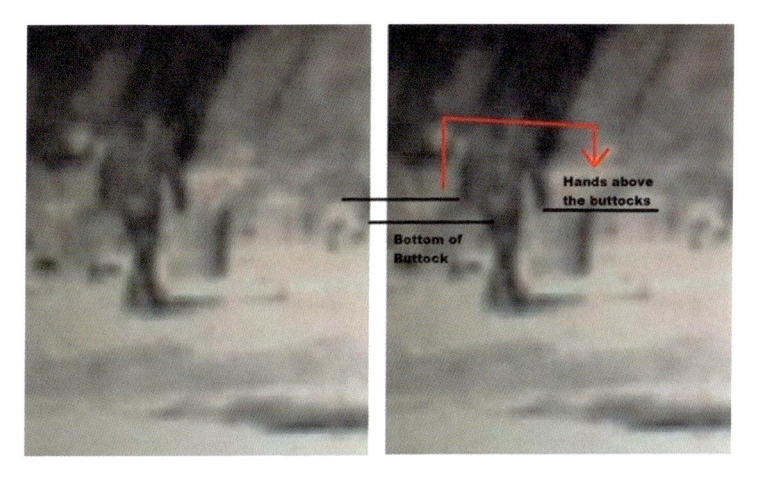

In the film when the Bigfoot is walking upright, we see the fingertips of the Bigfoot just above the lower buttocks, the same position as a man walking upright.

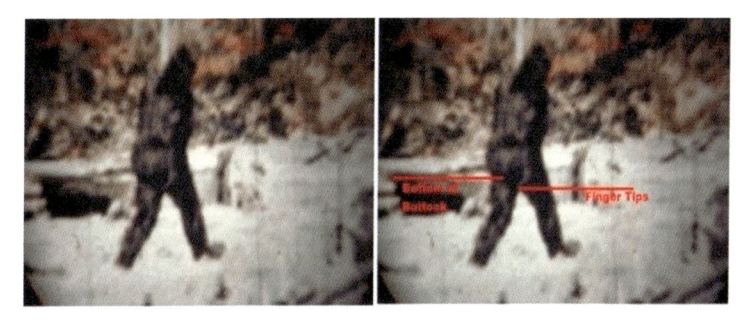

When the Bigfoot slumps over just a little, the fingertips come just below the buttocks, the same as a man's when he walks slumped over.

Test Image

With a costume, and as it is with my own hand-constructed Bigfoot costume, a set of shoulder pads inserted under the shoulders of the costume add three to four inches in height to the upper arm.

One can see the outlines of shoulder pads in images of Patterson's Bigfoot. These telltale pads appear to lengthen the arms.

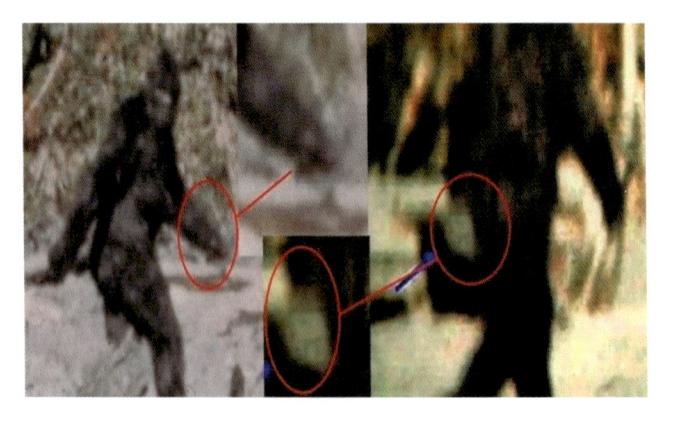

138

In the P/G film, we see the left hand open and close five times. This proves there were no arm extensions used in the suit.

Even in my test images of my suit, the man in the suit (Tim Beckholt) has the same length of arms as the creature in the film.

There is one more intriguing piece of evidence inferring that the P/G Bigfoot was not a Bigfoot. No one to my knowledge has viewed this overlooked piece of film. The image below is from the beginning of that film.

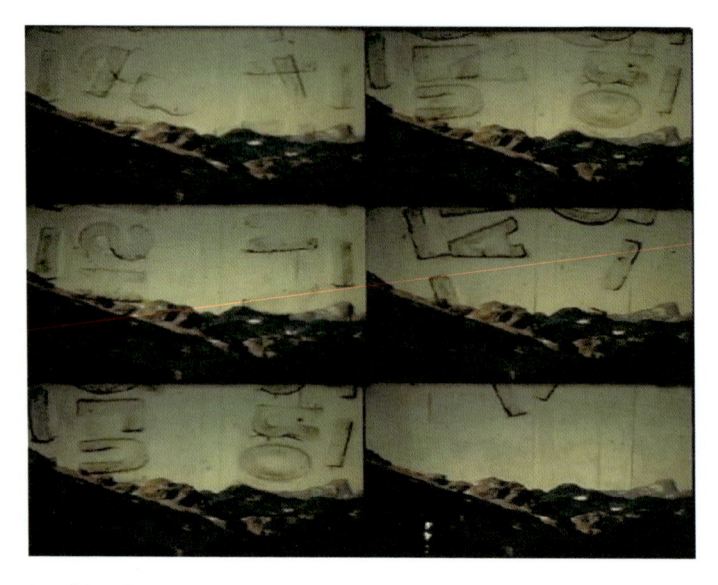

The film is approximately four minutes long and was shot in British Columbia by Roger Patterson. The film shows mountainsides and various scenery. In the film, a woman is holding up tribal masks.

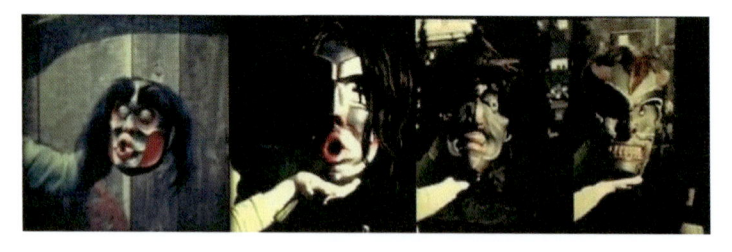

I provide here close-ups of the head piece a female is holding. I have blanked out the female holding the mask. The film includes top, side, and bottom true views of each of these head pieces.

It appears that Patterson filmed each head piece from all sides to aid him in sculpting heads. Taking such photos would also help in making masks. My contention is that Roger Patterson used details from these tribal masks to make the head piece for his Bluff Creek Bigfoot.

The film was developed in British Columbia as you can see the stamp at the beginning of the film.

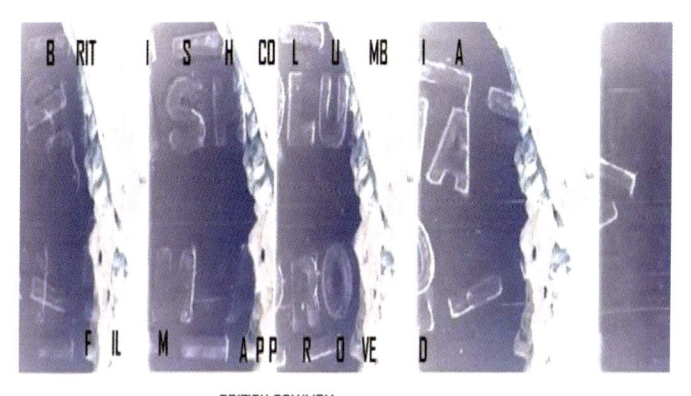

BRITISH COLUMBIA
FILM APPROVED

At the end of the film, the female that was holding the head pieces for Roger can be seen again.

I looked over the film to find out the location were the film was shot. And by lining up what can be seen in the film I found the location where Roger had filmed was the totem poles in British Columbia Canada.

Chapter Eight: My copy of the Suit

After closely examining the features of the suit Patterson used in the Bluff Creek film, I decided to acquire two commercially available gorilla suits. My plan was to use them to make a copy of the P/G Bigfoot suit and to compare the appearance of the copy as a man, Bob Heironimus, walked inside it to the appearance of the Bigfoot suit when a man walked in it at Bluff Creek.

One of the test images.

With one of the gorilla suits in hand, I re-reviewed the story Bob Heironimus told in which he described the suit he wore and his actions as he walked in the suit at Bluff Creek. Heironimus claimed that Patterson used pillows for padding and shoulder pads to widen the shoulders of the Bigfoot, which in turn gave the impression of longer-then-normal arms. I had a friend take pictures of me in the gorilla suit; I call these "test images." The image presented here (above) shows the appearance of the suit before I altered it to make it look like Patterson's Bigfoot suit. The zipper is sewn into the back of the suit, and the large size of the buttocks results from sewing two pillows to the inside the suit.

My test walks I the gorilla suit demonstrated that there are features that match similar features in the Bluff Creek suit. Notice that the leg and calf of the gorilla suit is similar to the leg and calf of the Bluff Creek suit. The backs and buttocks of both suits are the same. However, there are some differences in some features.

Bob Heironimus stated that he had his car keys in his pocket when he was walking in Patterson's suit. The accompanying image shows what appears to be, for lack of a better term, a hernia in the leg of the Bluff Creek suit.

In my test walk, the car keys I put in my pocket form an obvious bulge in the leg just as in the Bluff Creek suit.

I remind the reader that these test images were taken with me walking in the gorilla suit before I altered it.

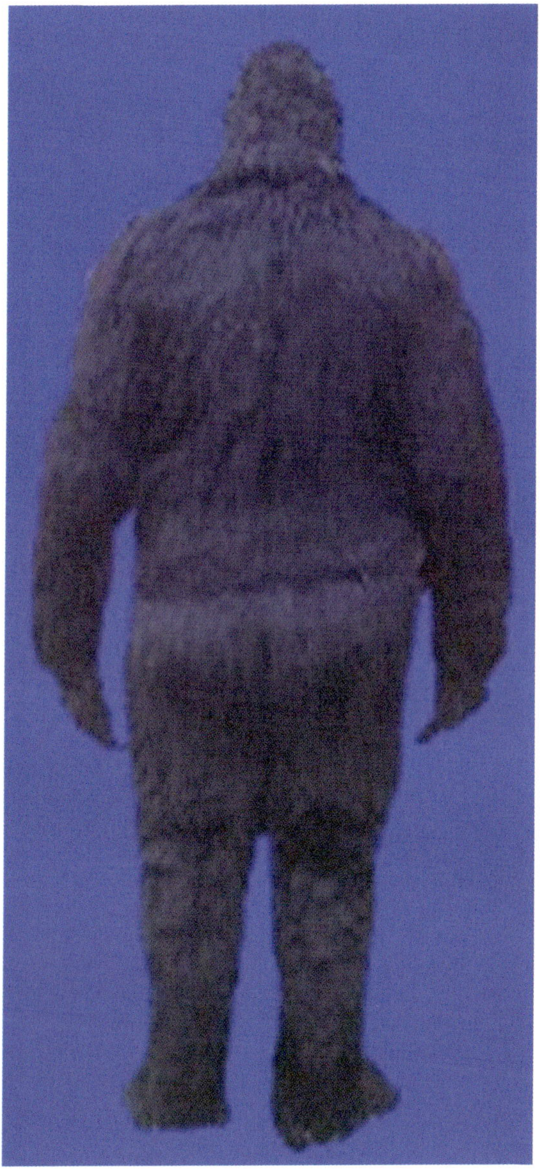

As we see in this test image, the fur is long. When I made the copy of the Buff Creek suit, I had to cut the hair on the suit to make it one-inch long (the hair of the gorilla suit was about three inches long).

If one finds these first test images on the Web or in a video, remember that those images show preliminarily that I could mimic the Bluff Creek Bigfoot suit in three features: buttocks size, shoulder width, and a protruding form ("hernia") in the upper leg. I took a store-bought gorilla suit—and added to it pillows and pads, and put car keys in my pocket, to achieve the bulk and width Patterson desired. (I don't think Patterson considered giving the Bigfoot a "hernia;" rather, the keys were a mistake—Heironimus should have kept them out of his pants pocket.)

After my preliminary tests, I took three days off of work and altered the suit as if it was made of bear hide.

As I point out, there were three men involved in the making of Patterson's original suit. Roger Patterson made the head piece; Ray Wallace made the feet; and Bob Titmus made the body. I spent six months studying the science and art of taxidermy. I then altered the suit in the manner I theorized Patterson, Wallace, and Titmus did.

Note:

Before I continue, I would like to point out that the materials I used cost me only $243; and it only took me three days to make the copy. I make this point because Bigfoot researchers and bloggers state that my replica of Patterson's suit cost me thousands of dollars and ten years to make. This is completely false. The Bigfoot researchers and bloggers spun this story from thin air to hide the real truth of the P/G film Bigfoot—that the Bluff Creek Bigfoot is merely a man inside a suit.

Test image on the height of a man in a suit/costume.

Before I made the replica suit, I made a test head piece and feet pads. I did this to find out how tall a man would be when wearing the suit.

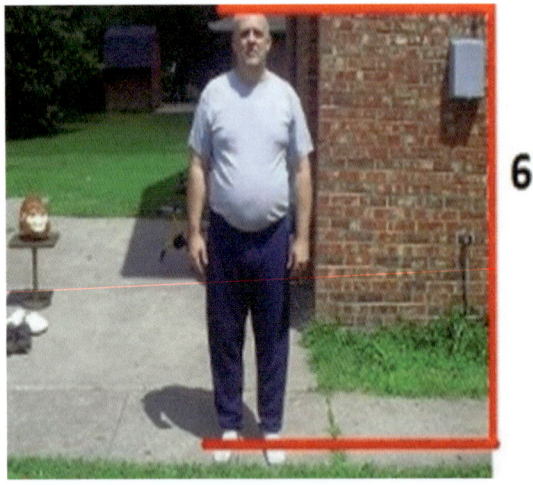

6'2"

Without the shoes and feet pads and the head piece, my height is six feet two inches.

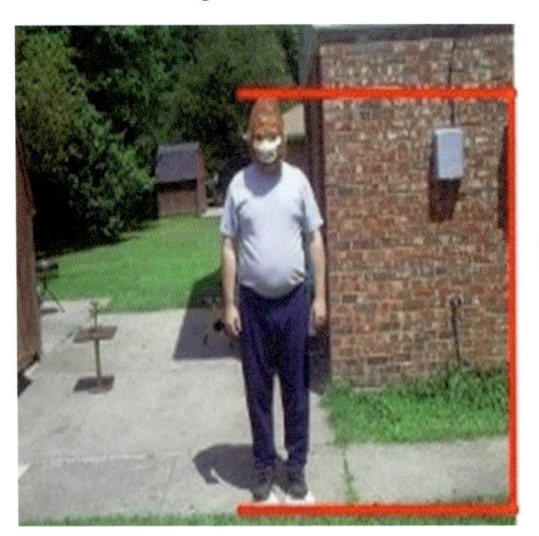

6'7"

150

With the head piece on, shoes, and feet pads, my height "grew" from six foot-two to six foot-seven.

Therefore, the shoes, feet pads, and head piece add an *extra five inches* to the "Bigfoot."

In the tracking dog film, one of the men in the film was about six foot-seven. If he wore Patterson's Bigfoot suit, he would stand seven feet tall.

The first step in constructing my own Bluff Creek Bigfoot suit was to create the head piece.

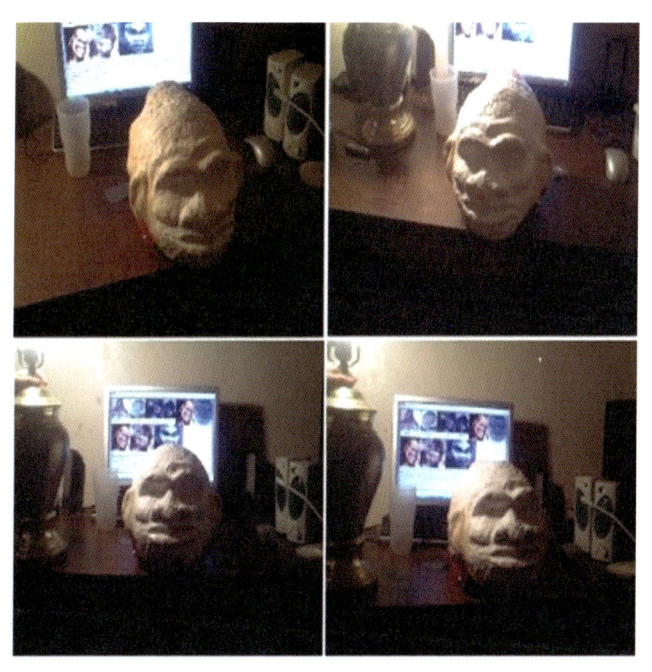

Images of the head piece.

When I was working on the head piece, I remembered that Patterson used leather; and that he made his head piece based upon the general shape of the tribal mask he filmed one year earlier in British Columbia.

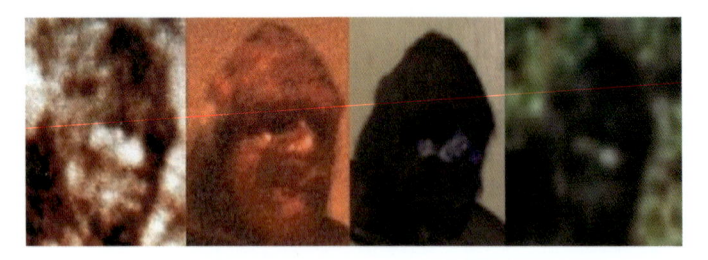

When finished with the head piece, I attached fur over it that I took from the gorilla suit I had bought. A side-by-side comparison of my head piece with Patterson's head piece in the P/G film reveals a match.

Side view of the head piece.

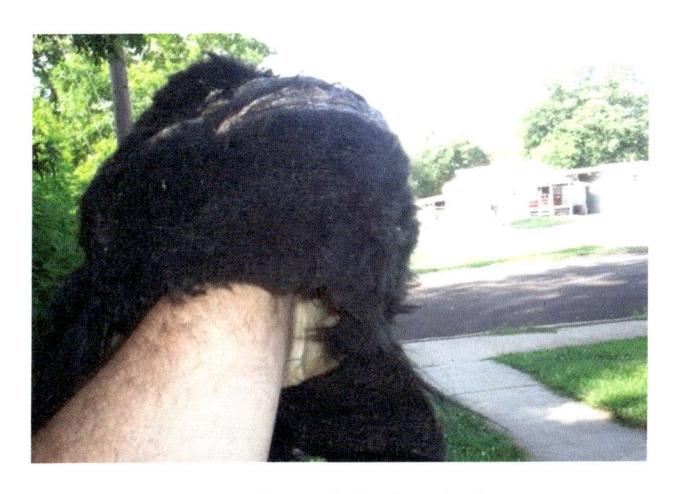

Bottom view of the head piece.

I made certain to have the fur on the head piece extend down behind the back of the head. In this way, the fur on the head would blend into the fur on the back of the "creature." No one could see that the head was a separate unit that sat on the creature's shoulders. And I made sure that the fur on the face fell down under the chin and blended into the neck fur and down into the chest fur.

With the face only seen for just a few frames in the P/G film (when the Bigfoot looked at the camera), no one can see the neck on the Bigfoot.

Zipper is in the front of the suit.

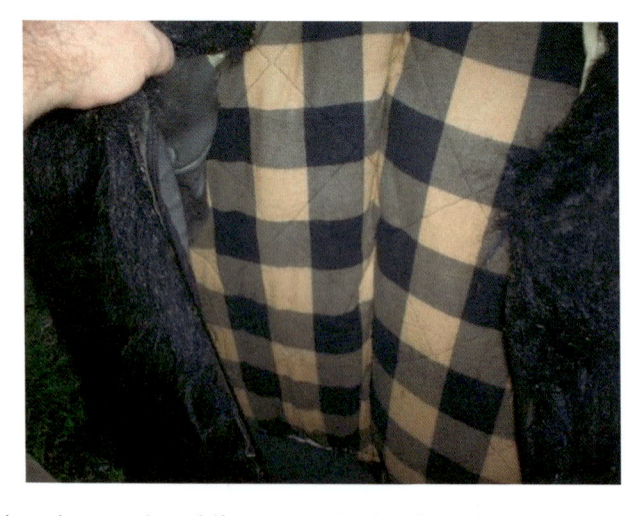

I hand-sewed padding onto the back and made a spine.

In this image, we see the "spine" on the creature.

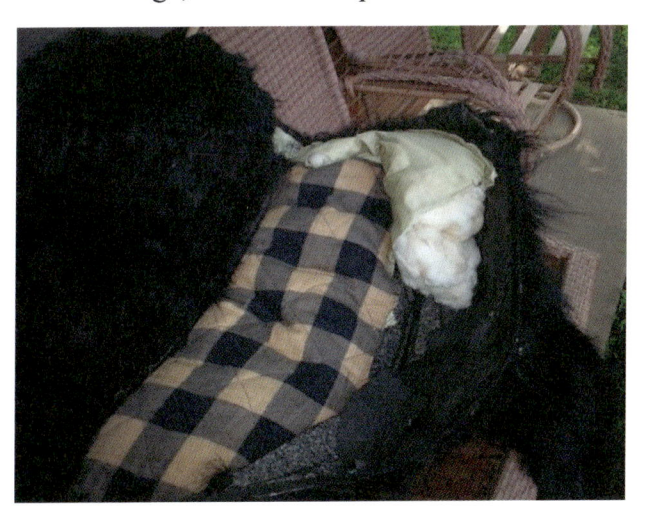

I then added padding to the shoulders. Bulking up the shoulders in this way allowed a person wearing the suit to move more freely in the suit without shoulder pads.

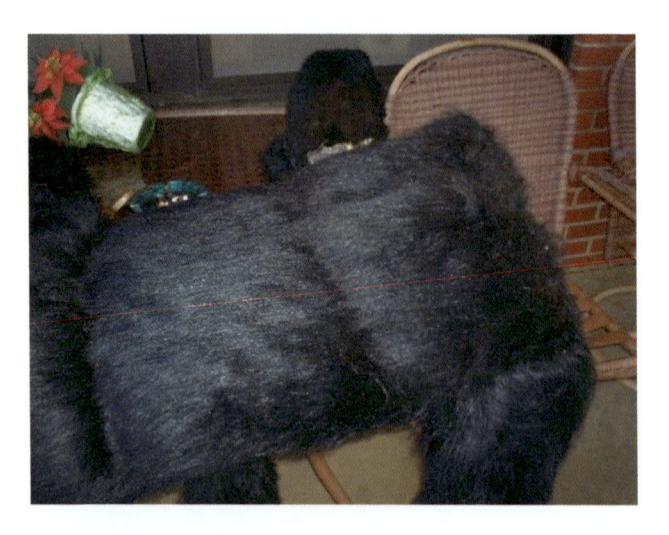

As you see here, when the suit is placed on the top of a table, the appearance is of a real body lying on a surface. The muscles in the body are clearly observable.

Padding added to form large buttocks.

156

Padding added to the lower part of the calf on the legs.

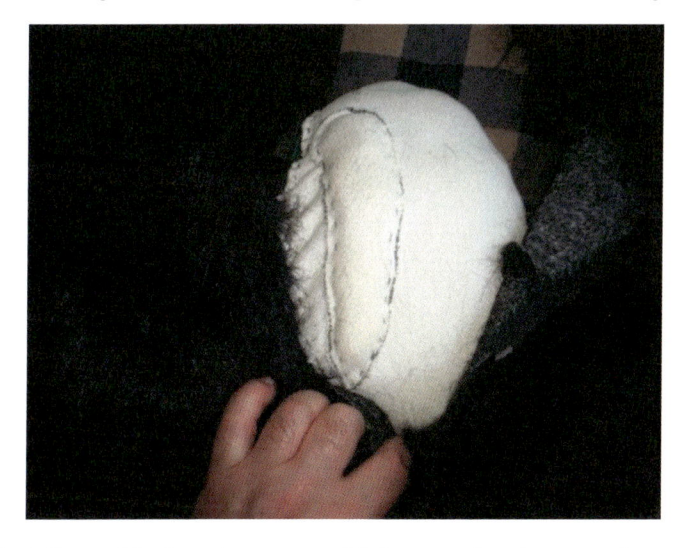

Padding added to the upper thigh to make the muscle movement in the suit natural (some people say they see a hernia).

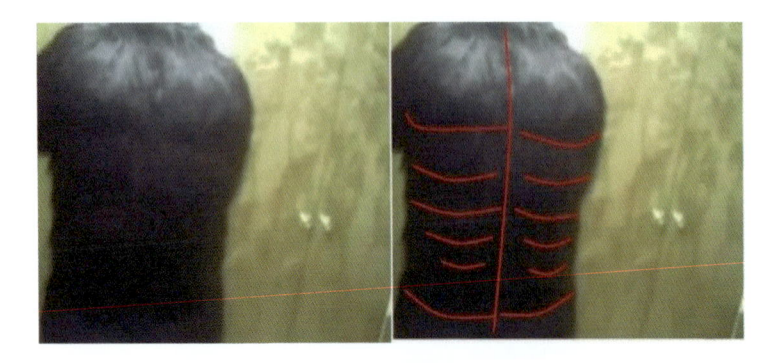

Test image of the back.

With the padding added, and me wearing the suit, the outline of ribs and shoulder blades is evident. A lot of natural-appearing muscle movement in the suit is achieved as a person walks.

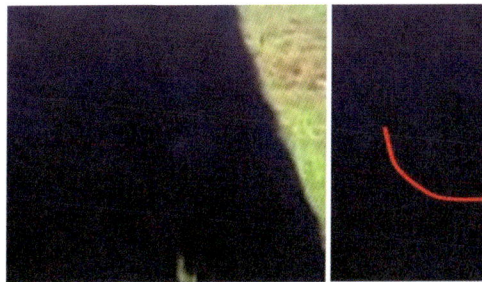

Breast.

After I altered the gorilla suit, I added breasts to the chest. I used the same shape and size of the breasts on an orangutan and added padding to fill out the breasts. This gives motion to the breasts when the costume wearer walks.

After I was finished modifying the suit, I took the suit outside and completed testing.

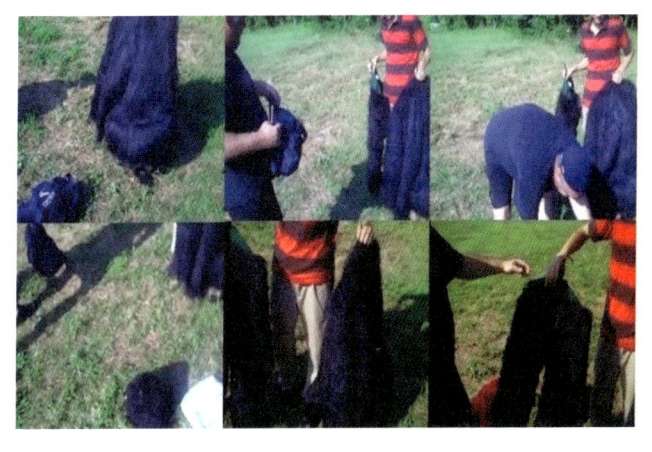

Test images of me getting ready to place the suit on.

The suit is made of two main pieces: legs and torso. I slipped my legs into the legs like putting on pants. I put on the torso like putting on a jacket. A strap I sewed to the lower buttocks comes between the legs and hooks in front of the suit. I then slipped on the feet, head piece, and hands.

Test image of me (Leroy Blevins Sr.) in the suit.

When I had the suit on to perform testing, it was 89 degrees on an October day. I wore the suit for more than 7 hours that day. I had to drink more than 4 gallons of water.

After the test, I was sick for two days.

In a second test, I wore the suit and walked in the manner Bob Heironimus did when he wore the P/G Bluff Creek suit.

Side-by-side comparison of Patterson's suit and my suit.

The Bigfoot that viewers of the P/G film believe is real is on the left; my suit—with me inside it—is on the right. The replica of the suit I made has the same shape and size as the Bigfoot seen in the P/G film.

Another side-by-side comparison of the two suits.

Again, my suit matches the Bigfoot.

The torso of my suit is the same shape and size as the Bigfoot in the film.

My head piece is not a precise copy, but it has the same shape and size as the Bigfoot's head in the P/G film.

162

Finished with all the testing, I contacted John Green. I showed him my research and images of my suit.

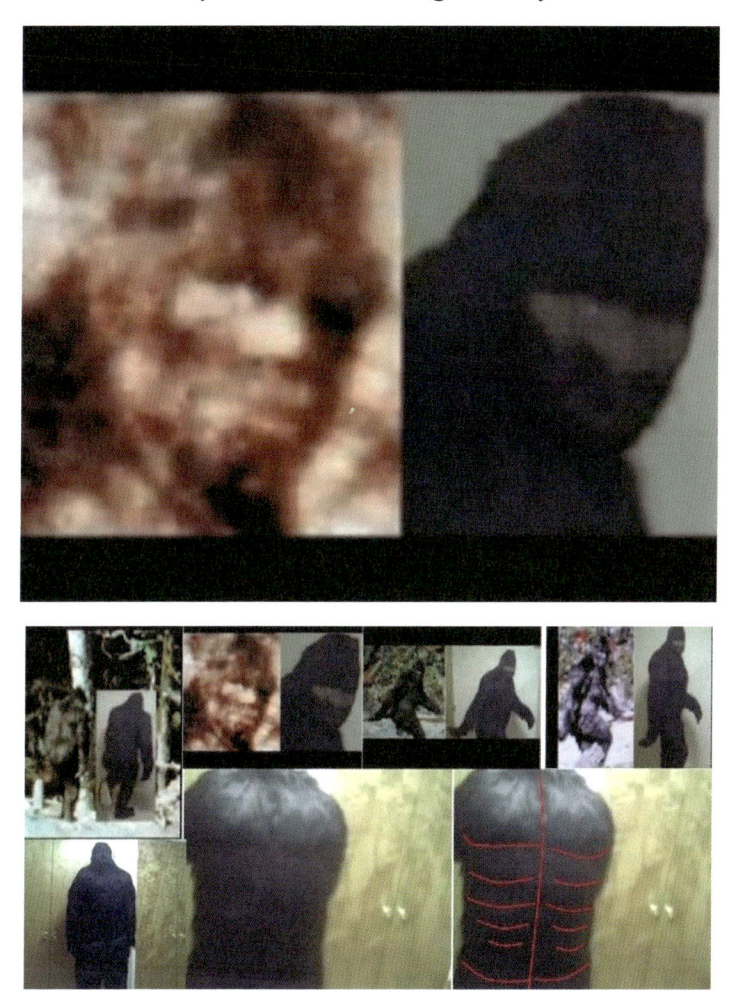

Images sent to John Green and parts of videos taken when I was in the suit walking and flexing the muscles.

163

John Green is the only researcher of those living in 1967 who were the closest to Patterson and who viewed the P/G film and declared the Bigfoot in the film real. There are two other researchers who were acquaintances of Patterson, but they remain silent about the film.

John Green commented in an email (transmitted at 5:51 AM, Saturday, September 18, 2010):

John Green: I am impressed with the effort you have made and the skills you have applied in doing it, in particular your costume, which is the closest to what the film shows that I have ever seen.

Green's statement is significant. It has been holy scripture for decades that no one—repeat, no one—could have ever designed and made a Bigfoot costume like Patterson's. Not Hollywood costume makers, *not anybody* on planet earth. This has been the "party line" for nearly 50 years. Surprise! I proved it can be done. It only cost me $243 in materials and three days to make a near exact replica of Patterson's suit. With further tweaking, I have no doubt that my suit would match to a level of precision that would convince even the last few diehard skeptics that Patterson's suit was a manmade costume. And I'm not even a professional costume maker; and I made my suit on the very first try!

Two other facts must be noted here.

Some Bigfoot researchers and bloggers like to show people images from the P/G Bigfoot film and compare them to a frame from a Bigfoot documentary produced by the British Broadcasting Corporation (BBC) in 1998. They inform the public that BBC tried to make a copy of the Patterson suit and failed. However, the fact is the BBC never claimed to have made a copy of Patterson's suit. The image of the man in the Bigfoot suit in the BBC documentary was used to prove that when a man in a Bigfoot suit is far enough away from the camera, no seams can be seen in the costume. But, naturally, Patterson supporters like to throw people off of the truth of the P/G film.

The second fact: costume-maker Phillip Morris sold a gorilla suit to Roger Patterson. It is my contention that Patterson never used it in his film. The Morris suit was used in another film, this one produced by Ron Olson of ANE.

Before I modified my gorilla suit, I performed tests on the gorilla suit to ascertain where the suit could have been used.

Ron Olson's feature film *Sasquatch - The Legend of Bigfoot* was produced in 1974. When I compared my unmodified gorilla suit to the so-called Bigfoot in Olson's film, it was clear to me that my gorilla suit matched Olson's Bigfoot. The texture and color of the Bigfoot fur matches the color and texture of Morris's 1967 suit.

At this point we will refer the Bigfoot suit as Patty for this is the nick name that researchers gave the creature on Roger Patterson film. Plus, they nick name the creature Patty because of Roger Patterson wife.

I like to take this time to answer a question I was asked after making the close copy of the Patty suit.

First I like to say the suit I made is not an exacted copy of the suit Roger Patterson used in his Bigfoot film. The reason why my suit is not an exact copy is because my suit was made with different materials then what was used for the suit in Roger Patterson Bigfoot film. I used two gorilla suits and Roger Patterson used a bear hid.

So at this time I like to explain on how the suit was made and how an exact copy of the suit can be made.

The Patty suit was made by 3 men.

The head piece:

The head piece was made by Roger Patterson. He made the head piece out of leather and he formed the face from a tribal mask.

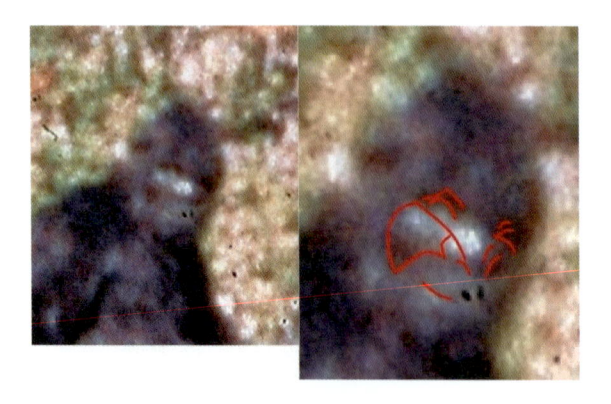

Outlines in the Patty face.

These are the type of tribal mask that Roger Patterson reproduce for the face of Patty.

Note:

This is why Roger Patterson filmed the tribal mask in B/C so he knew how to make the head piece for his Bigfoot.

Back on making the suit.

After Roger Patterson made the head piece he then places a gorilla dome on top of the head piece to make it look more like a gorilla. Then he places the fur over it.

The Feet or Bigfoot shoes:

The shoes for the Patty Suit, Ray Wallace made. He took a pair of the Bigfoot shoes he made and places the bear hid fur over them to make the shoe more like a boot so when the man places the suit on the feet will line up with the legs on the suit.

The torso and legs:

The torso and legs for the Patty suit were made by Bob Titmus. He was very good friends with Roger Patterson and John Green. Bob Titmus owned and operated a taxidermy shop in Anderson, Ca.

With Bob Titmus owning a taxidermy shop made it easy for him to have bear hid and to make the suit look more real.

The torso and legs are two different piece and they were not connected. The legs on the suit he placed muscles like padding in the inline of the inside of the bear fur. Then formed the legs into a pants like form.

The torso he placed padding in the buttocks area to form a bear buttocks, then place more padding in the upper shoulder area to form more like muscles and higher shoulders.

The back he places less padding and sown down the middle of the back to form what looks like a spine. He places the zipper of the suit in the front this made it easy to hide and for the man in the suit to put it on. Bob also placed a strap at the lower part of the buttock area to come up around between the man legs and hook in front. This way when the man walks in the suit you will the legs muscles will move in a different direction from the torso.

The breast on the suit he formed to look like a female gorilla.

As you see in the image above the distance of the chin to the top of the breast are the same.

Then he just added a little more padding to the breast to make them look fuller and real like a female.

Then just under the breast he placed a little more padding to push out the breast more and to give movement to the breast when walking.

This is why for the last 49 years no one can make replicated suit like the one in the film. They did not know what type of materials that was used and they did not know who made the suit.

By my research and my findings this is how I was able to make a close copy of the Patty suit.

Chapter Nine: Editing

For almost 50 years, researchers of the Patterson Bigfoot film have persistently overlooked a large array of facts that prove the film is a hoax, especially in the area of film editing.

The truth is there has been a great deal of editing of the film. Details have been added to the film, and details taken away. One clue can be found in the Library of Congress.

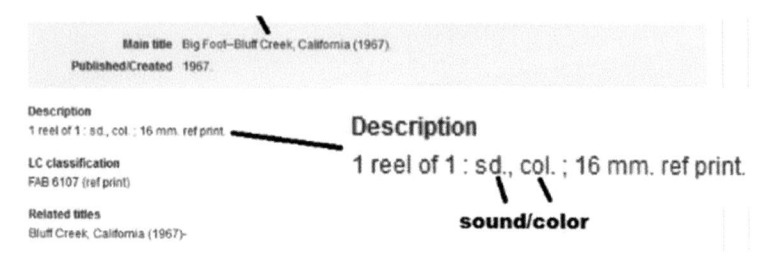

Main title Big Foot–Bluff Creek, California (1967).
Published/Created 1967.

Description
1 reel of 1 : sd., col. ; 16 mm. ref print.

LC classification
FAB 6107 (ref print)

Related titles
Bluff Creek, California (1967)-

Description
1 reel of 1 : sd., col. ; 16 mm. ref print.

sound/color

Records in the Library of Congress indicate that the Patterson film was one reel of color 16-mm film with sound. For the film to have sound, sound had to be added by someone in the film industry. Patterson shot the Bluff Creek creature and various pieces of footage near Yakima and Bluff Creek using a 16-mm camera without sound recording capability.

Information describing the P/G film (from the Web site IMDB.com).

Information on IMDB.com indicates that the movie starred Roger Patterson; Bob Gimlin was, supposedly, one of the directors.

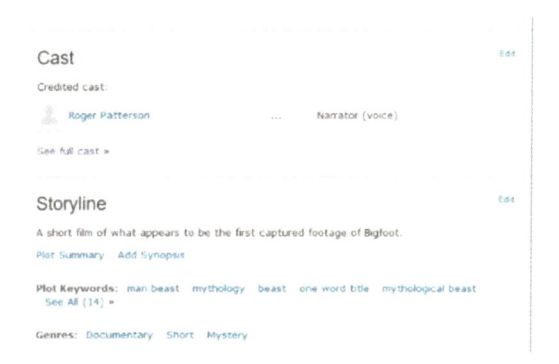

Other information acquired from IMDB.com indicates that Roger Patterson was the narrator. For voice-over narration to be in the movie, a professional film company had to be involved.

173

Information from other sources reveals that editing was done to the original movie.

Newark (O.) Advocate
Fri., Jan. 12, 1968

Editor Buys Film Clip Of Sasquatch

VANCOUVER, B.C. (AP) — John Green, a weekly newspaper editor, and Rene Dahinden, a lead salvager, said Thursday they have bought the Canadian rights of a 30-second film clip said to show an abominable snow woman, or sasquatch.

They said they bought the film, which Roger Patterson of Yakima, Wash., said he made in Northern California last fall, for $1,500.

The pair said they intended to use the film in a one-hour movie they are making in hopes of proving sasquatches do exist on the West Coast.

FIRST HISTORIC FILMS of LIVE CREATURE — A FACT!

Actual cast of creature's footprint.   Roger Patterson in "Bigfoot country."

BIGFOOT
"America's Abominable Snowman!"

Northwest Films brings you the first films ever taken of this creature, over 7 feet tall. Thrill to the excitement of the discovery of the tracks. Listen to renowned scientists discuss the BIGFOOT discoveries, filmed in part by the British Broadcasting Corp. in FULL COLOR and SOUND.

Life "..film is clear view of this creature"

Reader's Digest "..one of world's most intriguing mysteries"

National Wildlife "..150 year legend comes to life on this film"

TAKE THE FAMILY! — LIMITED SHOWINGS

Now Showing at the

5 More DAYS!   **CAPITOL** *Theatre*

OPEN 4:45   682-7044

Showings: 5:00 — 7:00 — 8:30

SORRY, NO PASSES FOR THIS ATTRACTION

Two newspaper clippings provide useful information. The first clipping, January 12, 1968, states that John Green and Rene Dahinden bought copyrights to 30 seconds of the film—these are only for Canadian rights that allow the film to be shown in Canada.

The 30 seconds of film show the Bigfoot walking. However, the so-called definitive Patterson film shown in full today is 57 seconds long. What Green and Dahinden bought were either edited portions from the P/G film stitched together, or Patterson added more Bigfoot walking footage later that extended the walking to 57 seconds.

In the *second clipping from 1968,* we see again that the film was in color and had sound.

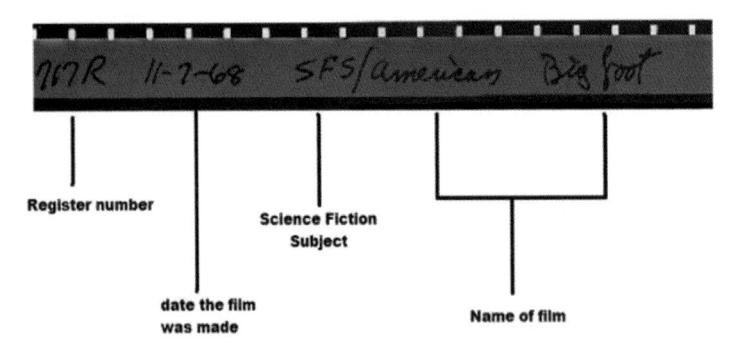

Register number

date the film was made

Science Fiction Subject

Name of film

The very end of the Patterson and Gimlin Bigfoot film

The image here shows the final strip of the P/G film at the end.

176

Marked at the end of the P/G film strip we see another date: November 7, 1968. This date marks when the film was remade.

Therefore, from October of 1967 when Patterson claimed to have filmed a female Bigfoot to the time it was edited, the Bigfoot walked from either 30 seconds or 57 seconds.

To find out who remade the film for Patterson, I started to backtrack through a series of facts.

In the summer of 1968, Ronald D. Olson was working at his family business, American National Enterprises (ANE), based in Salt Lake City, Utah. Olson also managed another company called North American Wildlife Research (NAWR) based in Eugene, Oregon.

In the summer of 1968, Olson contacted Roger Patterson about his film. Then, sometime that summer both Roger Patterson and John Green met up with Ron Olson. Patterson and Green gave the P/G film and other footage to Olson so he could remake the original Patterson film for Roger.

When Olson first viewed the film, he said the film was very blurry, including even the Bigfoot walking. He also noticed that the Bigfoot was on camera only 30 seconds. He asked Roger if he could fix the film: make the images clear, enhance the Bigfoot, and improve the sound.

A number of researchers claim that Olson and ANE had nothing to do with Patterson's film. They are wrong.

Image of Ronald D. Olson and the Bigfoot trap he made when he was managing North American Wildlife Research.

Ron Olson is in the left side of the image above. This image is from one of his nature films. The image on the right shows one of the traps he built when he was running the NAWR in Eugene, Oregon.

178

In the images (above), we see Ron Olson driving a Cushman in one of his nature films. Images also show Roger Patterson next to the Cushman. In the bottom left corner of the image, Patterson holding Bigfoot tracks, we note that the image was curtesy of Ron Olson. (Olson shot the image of Patterson when he was promoting the P/G film.)

In the image below, we see part of a clipping with words written on it by Ron Olson. When we closely study Olson's handwriting, we see that his handwriting is the same at the end of the P/G film.

Ron Olson company stamp mark inside at the end of Roger Patterson book.

Ron Olson promoted and sold Patterson's second edition of his book through Olson's NAWR.

Soon after Ron Olson remade Roger Patterson Bigfoot film in 1968. Ron Olson then started to promote Roger Patterson film and book.

How close was Ron Olson to Roger Patterson?

I contacted Joh Green.

John Green: Ron Olson became a good friend of mine and of Roger's and he was a very active and productive researcher for a number of years.

As I was viewing over the film I then looked for signs of altering in the frame. When I came upon frame 352 of the P/G film I found a small cut in the frame.

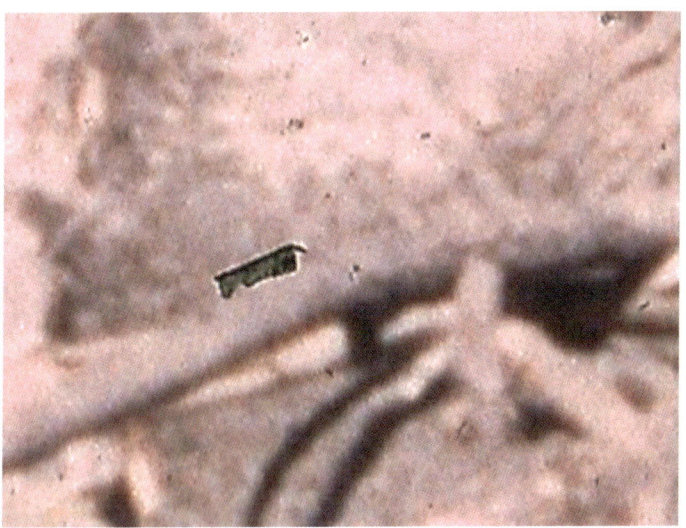

A color chart is placed behind a film frame to boost
weak color in the frame.

181

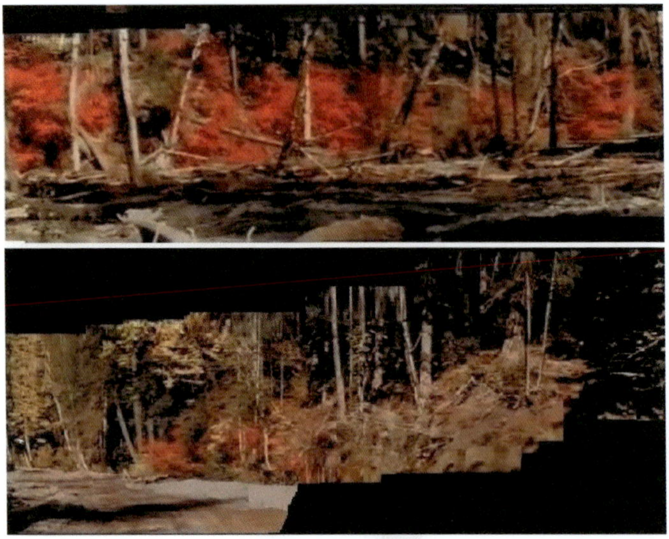

F
F
C
C

A green color chart was placed behind frames of Patterson's film to add more color and improve clarity.

By placing a film frame then a color chart over top another copies of the same film frame and place a different color chart behind it, you will get two different colors in the background and by using two copies of the same frame you can move it up or down in the back to clear up the front frame and focus it more.

The evidence I have collected shows that P/G Bigfoot film was in fact edited by a professional film company. Patterson supporters claim that Patterson shot in one take a clear, richly colored film in October of 1967. This is not true. Patterson's film was remade not only once but twice.

Original image.

Test image

If one takes an original image, makes a copy of it and places both the original image and the copy on top of one another, and then places different color charts between the two images and behind the original above image, the color of the top images will change and make the scenery in the film look more like the fall than the summer.

The first time the film was remade was in 1967. The work was done by an unknown company that edited together different pieces of Patterson's footage and added sound, making a documentary for him. Patterson also narrated the film. Patterson then copyrighted this film. Then, in 1968 Roger Patterson met up with Ron Olson. Olson remade the film documentary, added more scenes, a for the second time and added more scenes to it and cut out others. The result was a shorter documentary. It is hard to determent the true time frame of each film for they were remade a few time before the final film that we see today (P/G film). The time on this film today is 3:29 (3m.29s.).

Chapter Ten: Analyzing the Film

After investigating the background of the P/G film, which is complex and daunting, I knew what I had to do. I needed to develop a true, historic picture of how Patterson's original Bigfoot film became what it is today. The truth is that today's film has been cleverly manipulated to allow its moneymakers to develop a more "photogenic" Bigfoot and to heighten the drama of Patterson's "encounter" to persuade a gullible public that the striding Bluff Creek Bigfoot is simply cannot be an everyday man wearing a costume, but a real, living unknown creature.

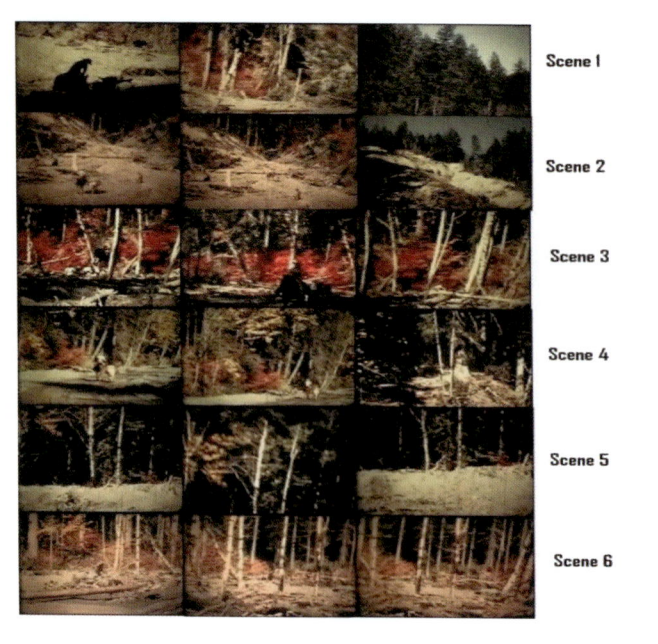

Frame from the P/G film.

The action I took was to place each scene from the P/G film in order from the beginning frame to the end of that scene frame. The most logical chronological sequence based on the physical movements of the Bigfoot. I then studied the color element in each frame and reshuffled the frames as necessary to develop the absolute sequence.

By lining up the color elements in the film, I discovered that scenes 1, 2, 4, and 6 all have the same color elements.

When I lined up the other scenes by color element, I found that scenes 3 and 5 have the same color elements.

This organizing process revealed that two parts of film were added to one other part of film. The scene of Patterson wearing the striped shirt was added to P/G film, and the first part of the Bigfoot walking was added as well.

Did Patterson film two Bigfoots?

Certainly with one film constructed of two different color element patterns, we know that Patterson's film was edited. Therefore, two different reels of film exist—both containing footage of the Bigfoot walking at the same location.

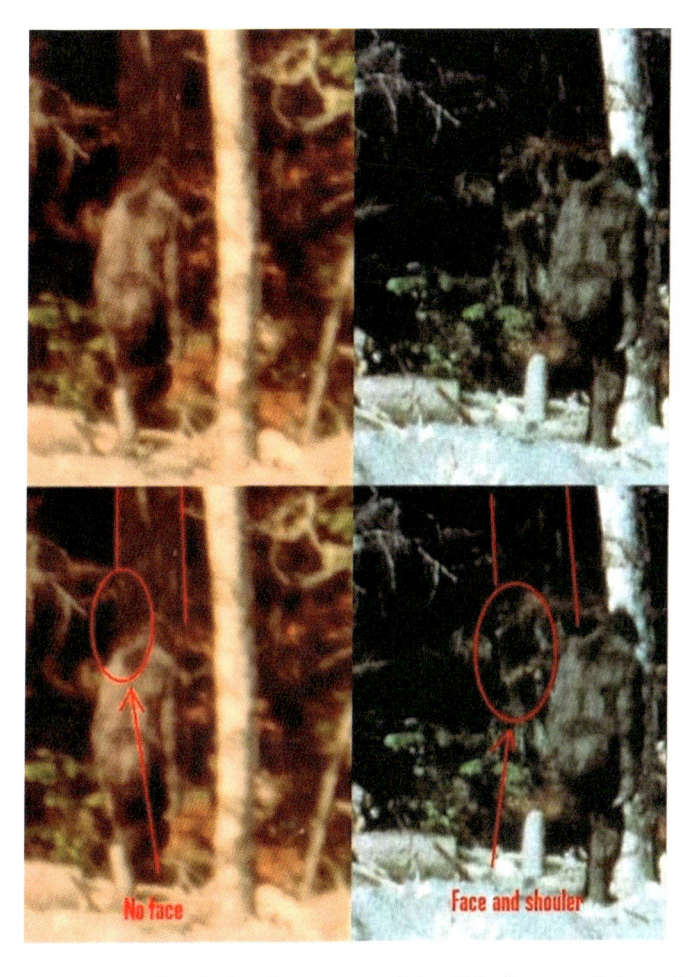

When I examined the first part of the Bigfoot walking, I detected a person standing behind some brush in the background as the Bigfoot passed by.

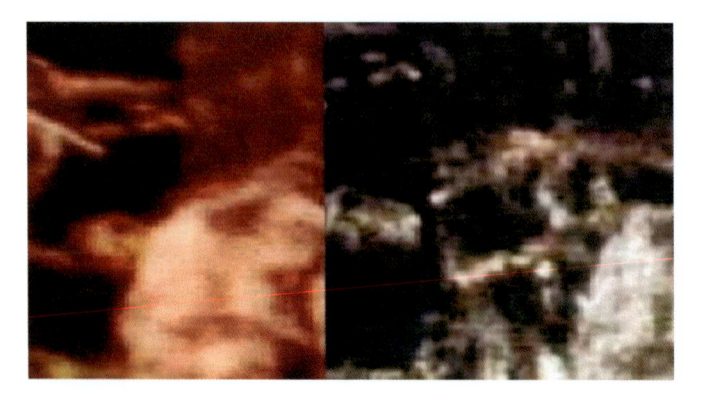

In the close up, we can clearly see the man's face. He is wearing a blue shirt. To find out his identity, I considered the "players" in the Bluff Creek filming.

When I laid an image of Bob Gimlin's face over the mystery man's face, I found myself looking at the face of Bob Gimlin!

190

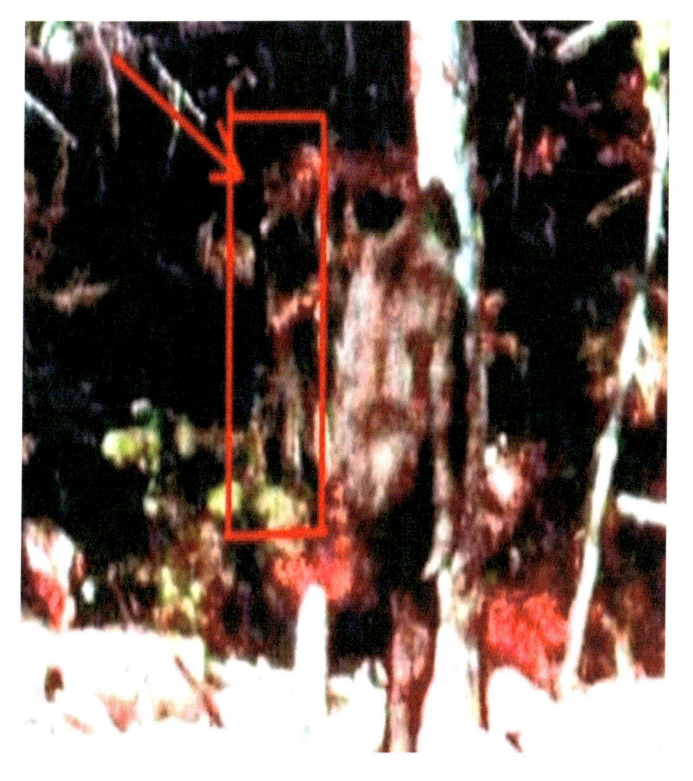

I added a bit of red tint to get a better look at Bob Gimlin behind the brush.

As the film shows, Bob Gimlin starts to stand up behind the brush as the Bigfoot is walking past him. As Patterson told the story, Gimlin was behind Roger, and Bob rode across the creek bed to cover Roger with his rifle. But here is Gimlin behind the brush as the Bigfoot walks past him.

I wondered why Bob Gimlin was behind the brush and so close to the Bigfoot.

Test images from my research.

In this test I place a camera man (Tim Beckholt) at the distance that Roger Patterson was from the Bigfoot. Then I got into passion to start to walk and place ear plugs in my ears to form of what it is like with a head piece on. Then the camera man (Tim Beckholt) starts to yell out action I could not hear him with ear plugs in like I would with a head piece on.

So in my next test I decided to place a man behind the brush and out of sight close to me. Then I place my wife (Tracy Blevins) as the camera person in the same location where the camera man (Tim Beckholt) was standing. I then got back into passion I was standing and then the camera person (Tracy Blevins) yells out action then the man behind the brush (Tim Beckholt) yells out action soon after the camera person (Tracy Blevins). Then I can hear the person behind the brush and then I started to walk. Then when the camera person (Tracy Blevins) yells out stop. The man behind the brush (Tim Beckholt) then yells out stop and then I stop.

By doing this test I found out why Bob Gimlin was standing behind the brush. You see with a head piece on the man in the suit cannot hear the camera man yell out action. But with someone close to the man in the suit in the background made it easy. For a man to hear action than a man that is over 80ft away.

When I published this theory several years ago, the response was: "There's no way that Bob Gimlin and the Bigfoot were 30 feet away from the tree Gimlin was near. That would make Bob Gimlin over 20 feet tall!"

After the bloggers started to make up excuses to disprove this evidence, I designed another test to determine how far away the Bigfoot was from the tree.

3 to 4 feet

5 feet

30 feet

My test showed that the Bigfoot was only around 5 to 6 feet away from the tree. That would place Gimlin only about 7 to 8 feet away from the Bigfoot. He was also elevated on the hillside. This is why Gimlin appears somewhat taller than the Bigfoot as it walked away.

If Gimlin were behind the brush, then obviously the Bigfoot was nothing but a man in a Bigfoot costume. Also, if a real Bigfoot was there that day, a man in such close proximity to it would risk being attacked by the Bigfoot.

Shown above is the cut in the P/G film that separates the first and second part of the Bigfoot walking.

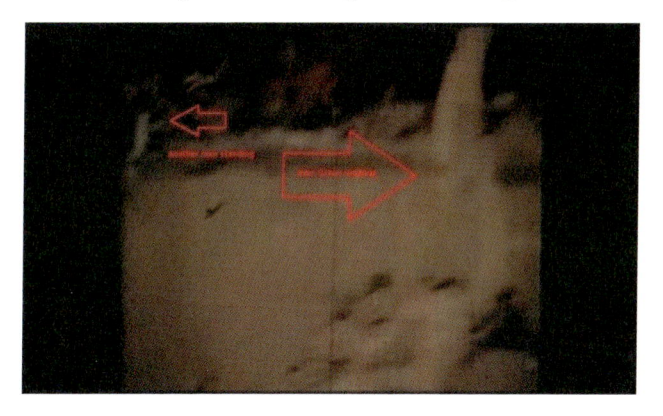

When looking intently at the second part of the Bigfoot walking, I noticed there were two objects taken out of the film.

Man taken out

Shadow of the man

In the film, in four frames a man was "whited out." However, his shadow still remains in the film. It was Bob Gimlin who was removed. I conclude this because Gimlin can be seen standing at about the same location where he is standing behind the brush as the Bigfoot walks past.

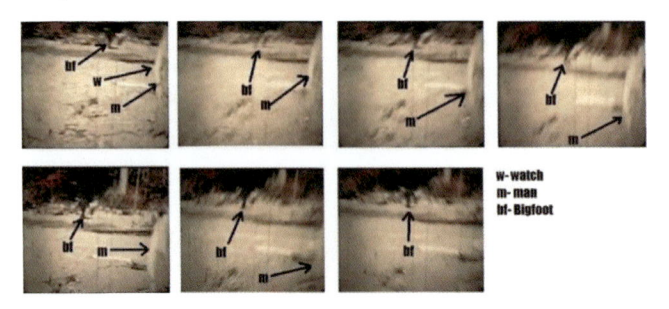

w- watch
m- man
bf- Bigfoot

In the next set of frames, at a point where we start to see the Bigfoot again in the film, an object walks in front of the camera and bends down out of frame. And in some frames, we see a watch and the outline of a man's arm.

196

A researcher contacted me and told me that the blurry image in this part of the film was an S-shaped tree (as marked in the image).

Close up of the S-shaped tree.

After viewing his analysis, I examined the S tree again.

When viewing the film in motion, the "blurry" image walks from left to right and bends down out of frame. Researchers claim this is a tree, but trees don't walk.

When studying the clear frames, such as the one above, the creature and all of the surroundings are quite clear. However, why does a blurry image appear—the S-shaped tree—when it doesn't exist in all the preceding frames?

To determine what the S-shaped "tree" actually is, I lined up the S-shaped tree with each frame that contains an image of the S-shaped tree. The findings were as I expected.

No Match

When the S-shaped tree is lined up with the blurry image, the blurry image doesn't match the morphology of the other tree.

After concluding that the S shape was not the S-shaped tree as claimed, I looked over other films that were taken around the same general time frame. In the tracking dog film, I found a man that in fact walked in this S shape!

Frame from the tracking dog film.

The S shape was matched John Green! When he walked, his body moved in an S shape. I laid the John Green frame in the tracking dog film over the blurry image. The result was surprising.

Match

John Green next to the blurry image.

John Green overlaid on the blurry image.

202

I found that the side profile of John Green matched the blurry image that was edited out of the P/G film. When in motion, John Green "walks over" the blurry image; the images are a perfect match.

Not only did Olson edit out Bob Gimlin standing along the tree line, he also edited out John Green who walked in front of the camera as someone (was it even Patterson?) was filming the Bigfoot walking. This fact places John Green at the film site with Roger Patterson and Bob Gimlin.

Not only was John Green edited out of the film, but the Bigfoot, which was supposedly walking continuously in the P/G film, actually stopped walking until Roger relocated himself.

Two close-ups from the P/G film.

Of the two close-up images above, the image on the left shows the Bigfoot when it is first seen in the second part of the Bigfoot walking sequence. Then, thirteen frames are inserted between it and the second close-up image shown above which is the point at which the Bigfoot resumes its walking.

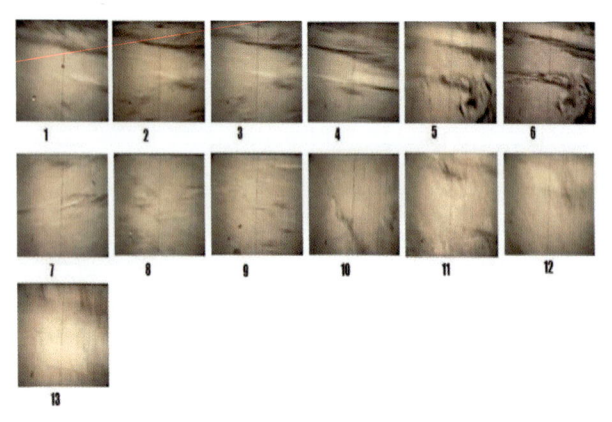

These are the frames that were edited in between the frames of the Bigfoot stopping and starting to walk again. This is when Roger Patterson supposedly fell to the ground. Or the so called ground sequence.

A viewing of this part of the film shows the Bigfoot stopping and standing still. Then, the ground sequence begins—when Roger relocated himself. He resumes filming the Bigfoot—and the Bigfoot starts to walk again.

stump ⇐

stump ⇐

Roger relocate

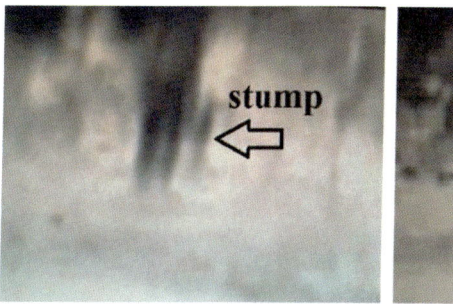

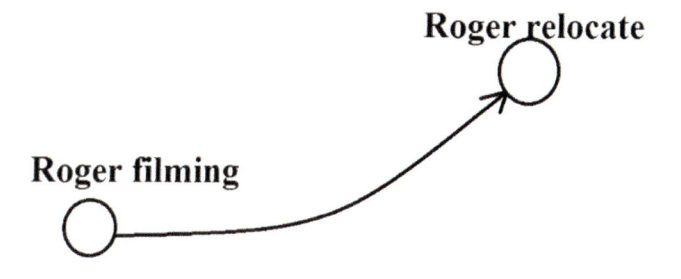

Roger filming

As seen in the diagram, Roger is right behind the Bigfoot, and then moments later, after the ground sequence ends, he is located more to the side of the Bigfoot. The fallen tree stump is marked in both of these close ups. If the Bigfoot did not stop for those thirteen frames, then the Bigfoot should have been past the stump.

Path the Bigfoot walked

Bigfoot track in the PG film

Roger Patterson filming

Bigfoot tracks in the tracking dog film

In this image above I like to point out something that is also seen in the P/G film and the tracking dog film. As it was told and by the P/G film and John Green film of Jim McClarin walking the path of the Bigfoot. This is the rout the Bigfoot traveled marked in red on the image above. But in the P/G film we can see a Bigfoot track right in front of Roger Patterson as he filmed the ground sequence. In the location marked in yellow. Even in the tracking dog film again we see these same Bigfoot tracks around the same location as seen in the P/G film. By the P/G film and tracking dog film shows us by the Bigfoot track as seen in the films. The Bigfoot was walking different routes there that day.

206

This is how the Bigfoot tracks line up. The Bigfoot walked two different paths as seen in the P/G film.

In frame 352 from the P/G film, I removed the Bigfoot from the frame to get a better look at the surroundings when I was analyzing both the P/G film and a film that includes local Willow Creek Bigfoot investigator Jim McClarin.

I marked a point on frame 352 where an object is clearly seen.

Close up of frame 352 showing an object.

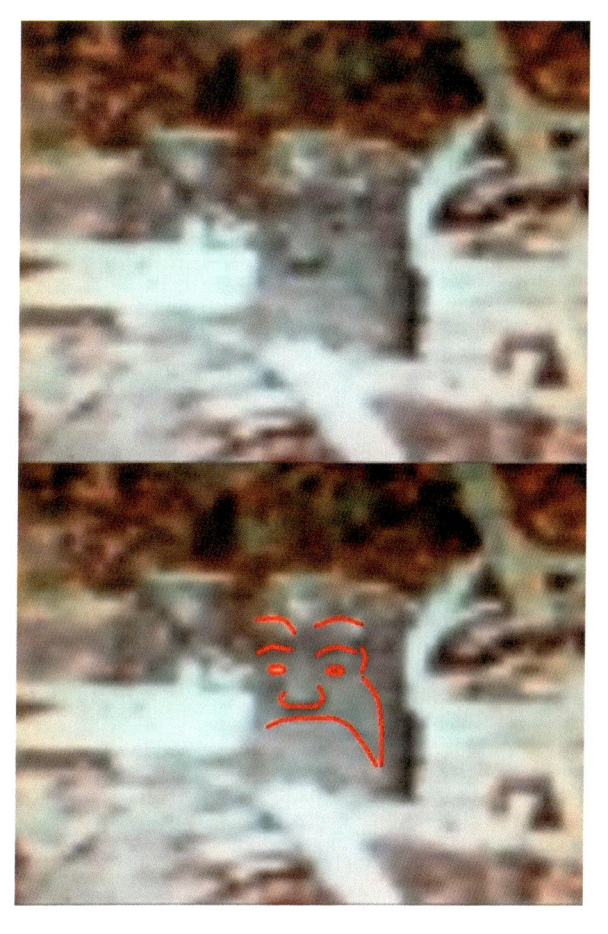

In 1967 when the P/G film was shot, Jim McClarin started to carve a Bigfoot statue in Willow Creek. In the P/G film, we can see that someone started to carve a Bigfoot face into a log that is sticking out of the ground.

Now, there were only two men who were capable of making wood carvings: Roger Patterson and Jim McClarin.

Another peculiarity in the Olson documentary is the presence of men on horseback. I studied the images in the film of men.

In the image above, Roger Patterson is riding the same horse that Bob Gimlin is seen riding in the film.

210

Later, I found Roger again on the same horse as seen in the film. This time he was wearing a blue shirt. When I did a side-by-side comparison of Roger Patterson and Bob Gimlin, I found that the man Bigfoot researchers claimed was Bob Gimlin was in fact Roger Patterson. Roger also went on expeditions in the Bluff Creek area and shot a lot of film there years before he filmed the Bigfoot. He talks of this in his book.

With Roger filming in the Bluff Creek area in 1966 while wearing a blue shirt, Olson simply added this early footage to the revised documentary and claimed it was Bob Gimlin when in fact it was Roger Patterson filmed one year earlier.

Facts on the films.

In 1967 Roger Patterson made a full documentary film.

This film footage has these cast members.

The stars, all from Yakima, who played in Roger Patterson's documentary (left to right): Roger Patterson, John Ballard, Jerry Merritt, Howard Heironimus, Bob Gimlin, and Bob Heironimus.

In this full length documentary film footage only shown the cast members and scenery.

Also in 1967 Roger Patterson shot a short film footage of a Bigfoot.

212

Both of these films in fact was done by a professional filming company in Hollywood Ca.

We can determine this by the films themselves because of the fact both films have sound with sound effects and a narrator.

Let us look only at the short film that has the Bigfoot on it.

But first let us look over some facts about this short film.

213

Film frame on the left is what I call the first part of the Bigfoot walking. The frame on the right is the second part of the Bigfoot walking.

The reason why I separate the two walk sequence is because in the original film footage the Bigfoot only walked for the total time of 30sec. This is why in all of the newspaper clipping and advertisements they done they laid claims to the Bigfoot walking for 30sec. in the film.

It was not until 1968 when the film was remade by Ron Olson of ANE that is when the first part of the Bigfoot walking was added to the film.

More as we go along.

After I discovered this information I then contacted John Green to ask him what was seen on the original film footage. John Green was one of the first people who have seen the original film footage.

I contacted John Green by email on Friday, September 17, 2010 at 3:30 PM. And I ask him can he please tell me what was on the original film?

The next morning on Saturday, September 18, 2010 at 5:51 AM I got a reply from Mr. John Green and he said and I quote,

"Much of the footage Is just scenery or someone riding, and both before and after the short clear section of the

214

creature walking much of it is just a useless blur, which presumably is why it is not shown commercially."

By John Green reply he claimed there is scenery and someone riding before and after the short section of the Bigfoot walking. By this claim place the Bigfoot not at the end of the film but somewhere in the middle of the film to have someone riding and scenery on both ends of the Bigfoot walking.

So in 1967 Roger Patterson got copyrights to the film. And by the copyright office and the Library of Congress there is 1 reel of film that is color and have sound.

In 1968 Roger Patterson turn over his full length documentary film and the short film footage that has the

Bigfoot walking to Ron Olson of ANE to be remade for Roger.

When Ron Olson was done remaking both films for Roger he kept the original films and the original mast copies films and gave Roger Patterson only the remade copies of both films.

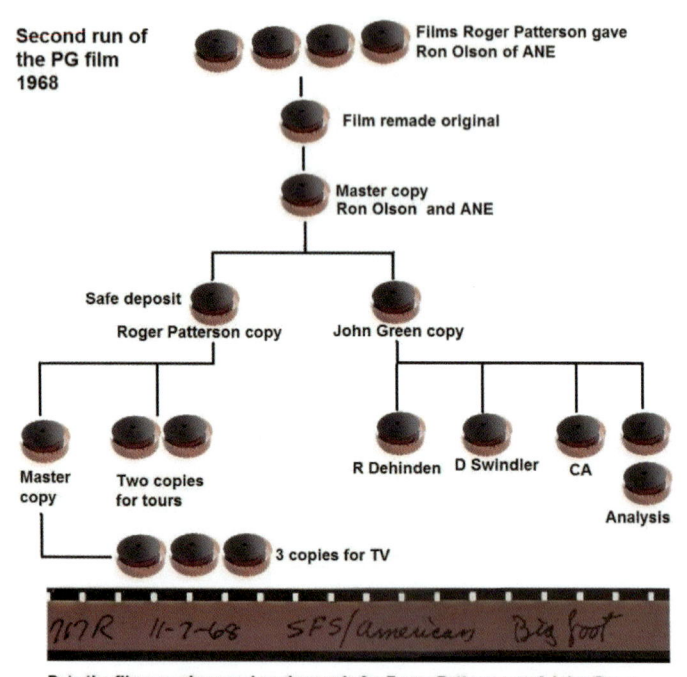

Second run of the PG film 1968 — Films Roger Patterson gave Ron Olson of ANE

Film remade original

Master copy Ron Olson and ANE

Safe deposit — Roger Patterson copy | John Green copy

Master copy | Two copies for tours | R Dehinden | D Swindler | CA | Analysis

3 copies for TV

Date the film was done and copies made for Roger Patterson and John Green.
Nov 7, 1968

Total copies of the film 1 original, 1 master copy and 13 copies = 15

Then Roger Patterson made John Green a copy and both men made more copies to give out and show on TV and their first copy of the short film they kept in locked boxes at their banks.

216

Chapter Eleven: When was the film shot?

Perhaps the biggest question of all is when in fact did Roger Patterson and Bob Gimlin film the Bigfoot? If they lied about the date of the filming, then the P/G Bigfoot film melts into a mass of useless celluloid.

When people talk about the P/G film, they never talk about the other films that were shot in and around the film site. We have looked at these in several different ways in earlier chapters. The films are as follows in chronological sequence:

1) John Green and Ren Dahendin tracking dog film.
2) The Patterson and Gimlin Bigfoot film
3) John Green film of Jim McClarin walking the path of the Bigfoot.

However, when it comes to all three films, Bigfoot researchers conveniently avoid talking about films 1 and 3 as listed above. They prefer to concentrate only on the P/G Bigfoot film, and of course believe that lucky

Patterson and Gimlin just happened to stumble upon a Bigfoot, and in one miraculous take photographed a Bigfoot walking leisurely in front of them.

As the story goes, the tracking dog film was shot first, in the summer of 1967. The second film shot, the P/G film, was shot in October of 1967. Then last film, Jim McClarin walking, was filmed in the summer of 1968.

Let's plumb the secrets of these three films.

As Patterson and Gimlin told it, they filmed the Bigfoot on October 20, 1967, a Friday. However, this isn't true.

In Patterson and Gimlin's story, they never mention inquiring of workmen who were cutting down trees if they had seen Bigfoot and where? Nor do Patterson and Gimlin talk about the trucks driving in and out of the road construction site all day long. Patterson and Gimlin say they filmed the Bigfoot on Friday, October 20, around 1:30 pm. This would place the workmen in the immediate vicinity. No workman has ever come forward to say they saw Roger or Bob. And, no reports of fresh Bigfoot tracks were reported being found after Roger filmed the Bigfoot.

Why would a Bigfoot risk be observed and possibly killed in an area filled with busy human activity? Supposedly Bigfoot is very shy and stealthy and attempts to avoid humans. Wouldn't the actual date of the filming be on a day when the workers were gone and Bigfoot felt safe appearing out in the open?

I decided to look for any reports of Bigfoot seen in the Bluff Creek area in 1967. Bigfoot tracks were seen in the area on September 5, 1967, the day after Labor Day weekend. All the workmen in the area left early on Friday, September 1,1967, to start their Labor Day weekend; they didn't return to work until Tuesday, September 5. Therefore, for three and a half days, the area was essentially void of people.

Could have Patterson and Gimlin been in the area when the work site was empty?

Box 152, Harrison Hot Springs
Sept. 7, 1967

Dear Bob,

Please excuse the stationery, there seems to be nothing else. I just wanted to let you know that footprints have started turning up again at Bluff Creek. They told me in February that tracks had only been seen about three times in two years, but there have been tracks of two or three individuals in the Onion Mountain, Blue Creek Mountain area and down on Bluff Creek a few miles above Louse Camp three times in the last two weeks.

Sylvester McCoy, who is now with the forestry at Willow Creek phoned me about the first set of tracks on August 23, and I rounded up a tracking dog and drove down, but the track was too old. I got home on Sunday, the 27th and the next morning a road contractor named Bud Ryerson phoned from his pickup to say there were fresh tracks made the night before. I managed to get $500 from the Vancouver Sun to fly the dog down and tried to get a man from the provincial museum as well, but none was available. Since I had a plane anyway I took Rene down--regretted it later, but that is another story.

There had been three individuals walk down the road, according to Ryerson. They went about 125 yards on the road, then followed the ridge past the old lookout on Blue Creek Mtn., then for the best part of amile, then were back on the road for 500 yards. The road is a new one and pretty well follows the top of the ridge. By the time we got there traffic had wiped out all the tracks in the travelled part of the road, but we still counted close to 600. There was the 15" track with the split in the ball of the foot that you cast on the sandbar and a 13" one with no remarkable pecularities. Ryerson said there was also a 12" track, but that was no longer evident by the time I saw them. My arrangements took too long and we did not reach the tracks until dark. The dog wanted to follow them and seemed very excited, but the handler would not. I didn't much blame him. Next morning the dog showed no excitement. It did appear to have the scent for a couple of hundred yards, but then lost it. Meantime I phoned the museum again and told them they were passing up the chance of the century, so they sent a man down, Don Abbott, an anthropologist. He did not get there until Wednesday night so saw nothing until Thursday, but he was convinced. He got five men from Humboldt State to come out on Frxiday, but when we arrived we found that the grader had wiped out most of the tracks, including three we had worked half a day on trying to soak in glue and make a cast of the actual ground. We had saved the best tracks for the museum people to look at, so did not get as good casts as we should have. There were also tracks down in the creek, the same 15 and 13, and on Tuesday there were 10½ inch tracks made at the same place below Onion Lake where the first set of tracks had been. These could have been a man, of course, only he would have had to be a regular barefoo walker to have gone where he did. Maybe a hippie. The tracks in the creek had gone through a trailer camp, and had been pretty well stomped out when I first saw them.

Letter written by John Green to Bob Titmus, on September 9, 1967.

John Green letter   Box 152, Harrison Hot Springs
              Sept. 7, 1967 ← **Date letter was written**

Dear Bob, ← **Bob Titmus**

Please excuse the stationery, there seems to be nothing else. I just wanted to let you know that footprints have started turning up again at Bluff Creek. They told me in February that tracks had only been seen about three times in two years, but there have been tracks of two or three individuals in the Onion Mountain, Blue Creek Mountain area and down on Bluff Creek a few miles above Louse Camp three times in the last two weeks.   **Sunday August 27, 1967**

Sylvester McCoy, who is now with the forestry at Willow Creek phoned me about the first set of tracks on August 23, and I rounded up a tracking dog and drove down but the track was too old. I got home on Sunday, the 27th and the next morning a road contractor named Bud Ryerson phoned from his pickup to say there were fresh tracks made the night before. I managed to get $500 from the Vancouver Sun to fly the dog down and tried to get a man from the provincial museum as well, but none was available.   **Monday August 28, 1967**
Since I had a plane anyway I took Rene down--regretted it later, but that is another story.

There had been three individuals walk down the road, according to Ryerson. They went about 125 yards on the road, then followed the ridge past the old lookout on Blue Creek Mt., then for the best part of a mile, then were back on the road for 500 yards. The road is a new one and pretty well follows the top of the ridge. By the time we got there traffic had wiped out all the tracks in the travelled part of the road, but we still counted close to 600. There was the 15" track with the split in the ball of the foot that you cast on the sandbar and a 13" one with no remarkable peculiarities. Ryerson said there was also a 12" track, but that was no longer evident by the time I saw them. My arrangements took too long and we did not reach the tracks until dark. The dog wanted to follow them and seemed very excited, but the handler would not. I didn't much blame him. Next morning the dog showed no excitement. It did appear to have the scent for a couple of hundred yards, but then lost it. Meantime I phoned the museum again and told them they were passing up the chance of the century, so they sent a man down, Don Abbott, an anthropologist. He did not get there until Wednesday night so saw nothing until Thursday, but he was convinced. He got five men from Humboldt State to come out on Friday, but when we arrived we found that the grader had wiped out most of the tracks, including three we had worked half a day on trying to soak in glue and make a cast of the actual ground. We had saved the best tracks for the museum people to look at, so did not get as good casts as we should have. There were also tracks down in the creek, the same 15 and 13, and on Tuesday there were 10½ inch tracks made at the same place below Onion Lake where the first set of tracks had been. These could have been a man, of course, only he would have had to be a regular barefoot walker to have gone where he did. Maybe a hippie. The tracks in the creek had gone through a trailer camp, and had been pretty well stomped out when I first saw them.   **Line talked about Bob Titmus**

Don Abbott got there on Wednesday August 30, 1967

5 men got there on Friday Sept 1, 1967

Note: Jim McClarin was 1 of the men from Humboldt State that came down there on Sept. 1, 1967

Note 2: In the letter it talked about the cast print Bob Titmus made on the sandbar it was a 15" track. Bob Titmus was not there so how did he made a cast print on the sandbar?

A letter written by John Green to Bob Titmus reveals when John Green was in the Bluff Creek area. It was on that date that Green or others shot the tracking dog film. The letter states that John Green and Rene Dahinden arrived in the Blue Creek Mountains on Monday, August 28, 1967.

221

In the letter, Green talks describes his activities in Bluff Creek and how he soaked one of the Bigfoot tracks he discovered with glue.

> we found that the grader had wiped out most of the tracks, including three we had worked half a day on trying to soak in glue and make a cast of the actual ground. We had saved the best tracks for the museum people to look at, so did not get as good casts as we should have. There were also tracks down in the creek, the same 15 and 13, and on Tuesday there were 10½ inch tracks made at the same place belo

John Green

Don Abbott

Note:
Location: Blue Creek Mountain

The images of the glued tracks support Green's story of his activities.

> the travelled part of the road, but we still counted close to 600. There was the 15" track with the split in the ball of the foot that you cast on the sandbar and a 13" one with no remarkable peculiarities. Ryerson said there was also a 12" track, but that was no longer

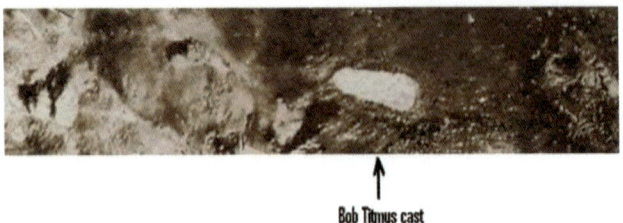

↑
Bob Titmus cast

222

In the letter, Green also talks about Bob Titmus's cast he made in the sand bed. This is the cast print that Roger Patterson claimed he had made; it is included in his first documentary. Roger did not shoot film of this cast, nor did he make the cast. The cast was made, in fact, by Bob Titmus.

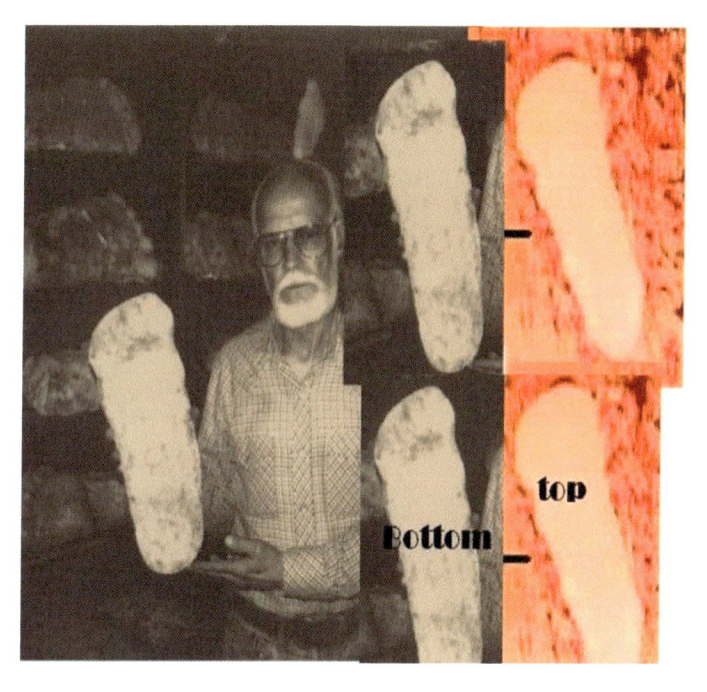

The image above is of one of the cast prints Bob Titmus made in the Bluff Creek area in 1967. It was falsely claimed that Patterson made the cast.

Strip of film from the original tracking dog film (shot by Rene Dahinden).

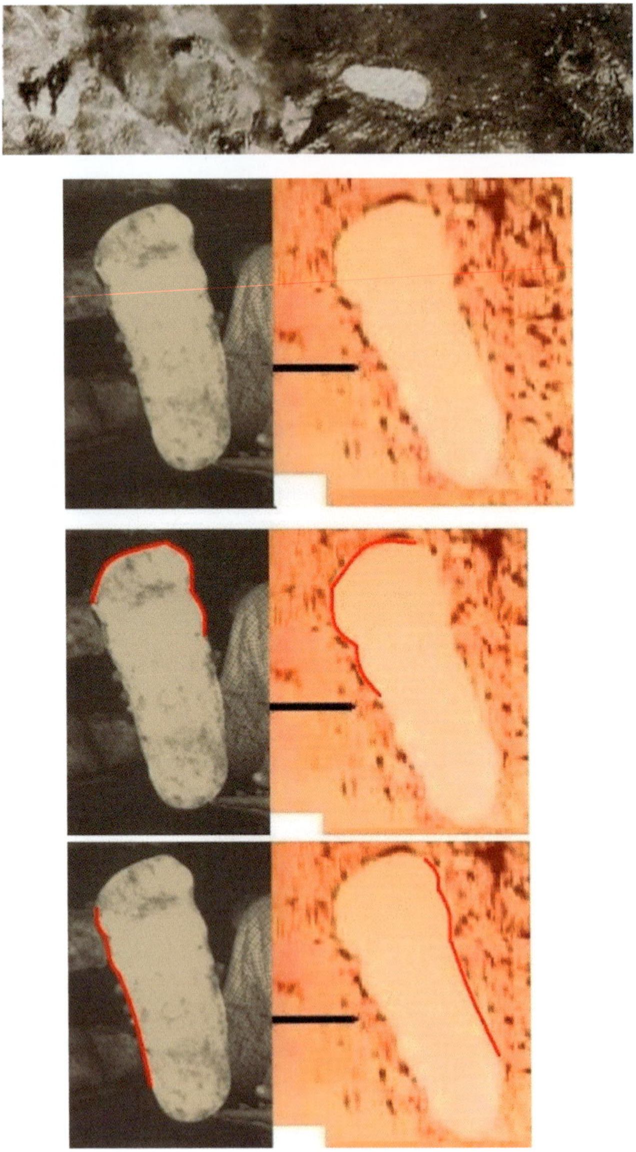

The cast print shown in Bob Titmus's hand has the same shape and size as the cast print seen in a short sequence in the film of the cast print in the sand bed. Titmus is holding the cast with the heel oriented down and the top of the foot pointed up. Identification that the cast he is holding is the same as the cast in the sand bed is made by comparing the outlines of the form of the cast.

In Green's letter, we also see that Don Abbott a British Columbia Archaeologist, who was the curator of Archaeology at the Royal B.C. Museum from 1960 until 2000. Arrived in the Bluff Creek area on Wednesday, August 30, 1967. On Friday, September 1, 1967, five men from Humboldt State University that was located in Eureka Ca. also traveled to Bluff Creek. Green's letter with all this information places John Green and Rene Dahendin in the Bluff Creek area on that Labor Day weekend.

Two frames above are from the tracking dog film show two of the men from Humboldt State. (One of the men from Humboldt State was Jim McClarin.)

Frame from John Green's film shows Jim McClarin walking the path of the Bigfoot.

John Green with dog called White Lady at Bluff Creek 1967.

In Green's letter he also talked about the tracking dog he and Dahinden took with them.

Image of John Green with the tracking dog, White Lady. White Lady appears in the tracking dog film.

Keith Chiazzari, the pilot that flew Green and Dahinden (and White Lady) to Bluff Creek.

Frame from the tracking dog film showing Keith Chiazzari.

Keith Chiazzari, pilot, appears in the tracking dog film. He was walking around with a rifle. Some researchers claimed this was Bob Titmus, but the man was indeed the pilot that flew John Green down on August 28, 1967.

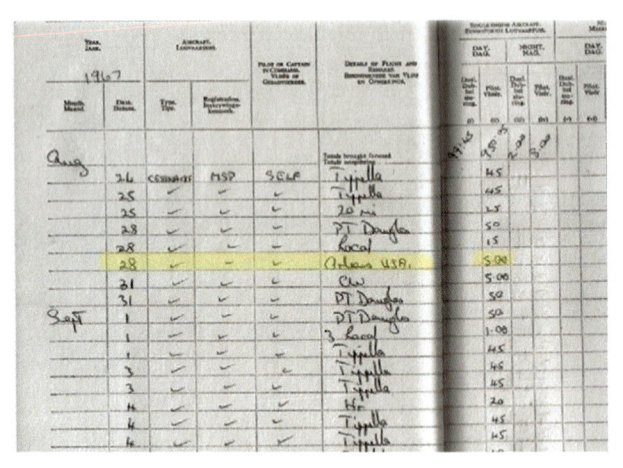

Scan copy of Keith Chiazzari's flight log.

Keith Chiazzari left Bluff Creek; John Green and Rene Dahinden stayed. Dale Moffitt was also at Bluff Creek.

Dale Moffitt is seen holding the tracking dog.

Green's letter and the tracking dog film and photographs that support his letter place Green and Dahinden in the Bluff Creek area on the last week of August and Labor Day weekend. As I point out, the last report of Bigfoot tracks found in that area was on Tuesday, September 5, 1967, the day after the three-day Labor Day weekend when the workmen returned to work and found three sets of Bigfoot tracks.

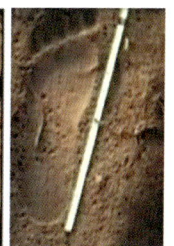

229

In his letter Green states that these tracks were made on the last weekend of August, and that the tracks were almost gone when he arrived at the site. Monday, August 28,1967

In the tracking dog film, the images of tracks show them to be freshly made, not almost gone.

Using the dates that the tracking dog film was shot—on Labor Day weekend, September 2-3, and the Monday following, September 4th 1967 I was able to determine when the P/G film was shot. With the workmen gone for these three days, the tracking dog film would have been shot unimpeded by the activities of the work crews.

As Patterson stated, he and Gimlin were in the area of Mount St. Helens at the same time that Green and Dahinden were down in the Blue Creek Mountains of Bluff Creek. And as I point out earlier, Patterson and Gimlin took a trip to Mount St. Helens in 1965. By claiming that they were at Mount St. Helens, Patterson and Gimlin had an alibi that they weren't anywhere near Bluff Creek when Bigfoot tracks started showing up there.

It is important to remember: the only time a dog was in Bluff Creek was when John Green was there shooting his tracking dog film. In the P/G film, we can see one of the dog's prints in the sand.

Amazingly, in frame 352 of the P/G film, if one looks carefully at the bottom of the frame, one can see a dog print in the sand. The dog print appears in the frame when the Bigfoot looks back at the camera man. Researcher MK Davis was the first person to point this out. The print actually shows up in about four frames of the film.

The dog footprint looks fresh. With Patterson claiming the P/G film was shot in October and John Green in Bluff Creek more than seven weeks earlier, the dog print should have been badly eroded, if not gone.

With this dog print information, and knowing that John Green was edited out of the P/G film by Ron Olson of ANE, I suspect that Green's tracking dog film and Patterson's Bigfoot film were shot at the same time and at the same location on Labor Day weekend, September 2-4, 1967.

More evidence of a hoax can be found in yet another film, the Jim McClarin walking film.

Film frame of Jim McClarin walking the path of the Bigfoot.

Green and McClarin say the McClarin walking film was shot in the summer of 1968, one year after the tracking dog film and the P/G film. However, when I analyzed this film, I uncovered details that imply that it was actually shot at the same time as the other two films, tracking dog and P/G Bigfoot.

The track in the first frame of the Jim McClarin film looks the same as the Bigfoot track in the tracking dog film. If McClarin's film was created one year later (1968) than the tracking dog film (1967), then the tracking dog track should have been gone. However, both tracks are fresh and lookalike.

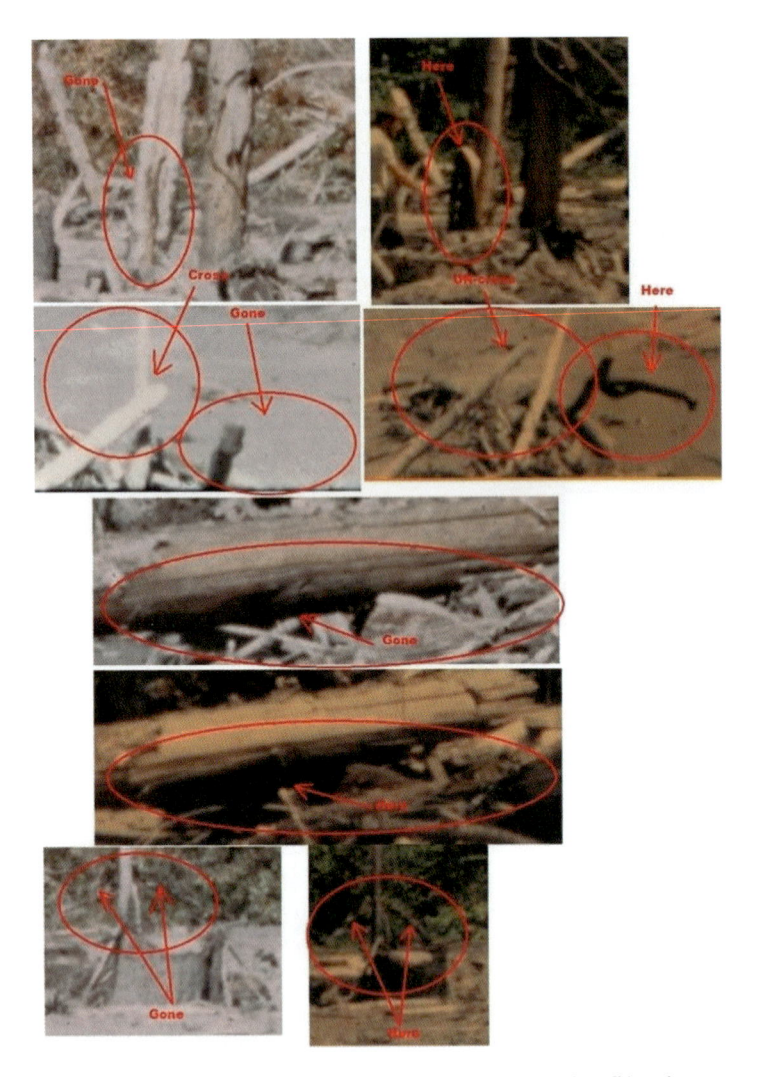

I zoomed in on the McClarin film and the P/G film in different location and compared its surroundings to one another. And I discovered several differences in the surroundings.

234

Close-ups from Jim McClarin and the P/G films.

Look at the locations I have marked on the two frames above. The Jim McClarin film was shot at the same time as the tracking dog film, and *before* Patterson's Bigfoot film was shot.

Look at the downed tree. In the McClarin film, bark is hanging down on the downed tree. But, in the Patterson film, the bark is *gone*.

Also, the extended branch we see in the McClarin film just as it is cut off in the P/G film. However, in both films we see the same dog print in the same location.

Thus, if the McClarin walking-the-path-of-the-Bigfoot film was shot in 1968, then the objects we see in that film should have been gone but still in place in the P/G film of 1967. However, we have the inverse: the objects in the McClarin film are *gone* in the P/G film. There are more of these strange reappearing acts.

In the Jim McClarin film, a big piece of bark is hanging over and around from the tree. However, in the P/G film (supposedly shot a year earlier) the piece of bark is gone.

From the PG film

From John Green film

Close-up of boot print.

From the PG film

From John Green film

From the PG film

From John Green film

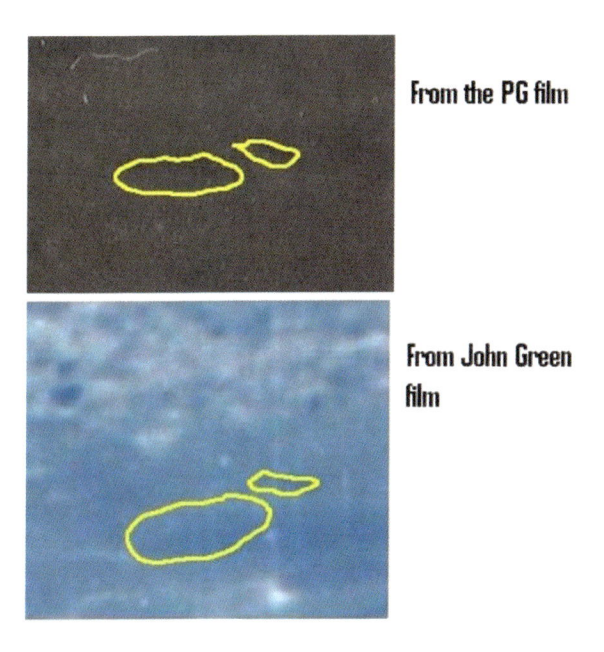

This boot print is seen in the same location in the sand bar in both films (P/G film and Jim McClarin film), which it is claimed were shot a year apart.

In the close-up of this area (shown above) from the McClarin film, we see not only fresh boot prints, but we see fresh Bigfoot tracks. Wouldn't Patterson's Bigfoot tracks have long vanished? (Recall that a storm struck Patterson's film site the evening after the famous Bigfoot filming.)

This evidence proves that the Jim McClarin film was shot *before* Roger Patterson filmed his Bigfoot. With this in mind, then how did Jim McClarin know the path the Bigfoot was going to walk?

After I found this evidence and showed it to Jim McClarin, he did not have an answer for me.

The evidence laid forth here shows us that not only did John Green and Rene Dahendin shoot the tracking dog film, but they also filmed Jim McClarin walking the path of the Bigfoot—and then helped Roger film his Bigfoot.

All three films were shot during September 2-4, 1967, on Labor Day weekend.

Another piece of evidence: The P/G film shows no leaves floating in the air or drifting to the ground. As a matter of fact, there aren't any leaves on the ground in the film, or on the road side or on the road itself. This is an important detail because pieces of footage shot by Patterson show fall leaves on the trees, which turn color only in October. Well, don't forget that Patterson also filmed scenery in 1966 in Bluff Creek; and he could have done so in October. That earlier footage most likely was edited into his documentary.

Images I took during Labor Day weekend of 2010 at my home in Cynthiana, Kentucky. As you see, there are leaves on the ground. Now if the P/G film was shot in

October as was claimed, then where are the leaves in his film??

Another fact I like to point out.

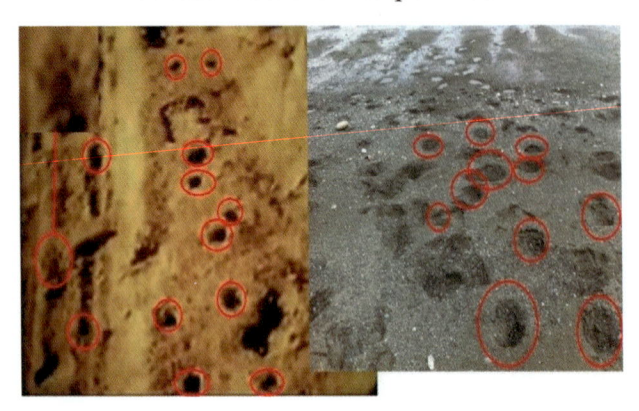

When I was analyzing the Tracking dog film I found that when they were filming the dirt road there is horse prints seen. And the dog print is seen.

In the image above on the left is a frame from the tracking dog film and the image on the right is horse tracks in sand.

And as you see the horse tracks in the sand are the same type of House tracks seen in the tracking dog film.

And the only men that had horses down there was Roger Patterson and Bob Gimlin.

242

Chapter Twelve: Who wore the suit?

Only one man has come forth to seriously make the claim that he wore a Bigfoot suit in the PG film. His name is Bob Heironimus.

He was immediately attacked by PG film believers, which still continue today. To prove his case that he was the man in the suit, he agreed to two polygraphs (commonly called "lie detector" tests).

Even after Mr. Heironimus took the test and passed both, he still was called a liar.

The skeptics state that Heironimus was not the man in the Bigfoot suit because he didn't not know how to get to the film site. Therefore, he wasn't at the film site. If his memory has failed him in this regard, we cannot discount his claim on the basis of this one item. It neither proves nor disproves his truthfulness.

If we say that Heironimus is a liar because of his lack of specificity regarding the location of the film site, we will need to call Bob Gimlin and John Green liars as well.

Even to this day, neither John Green or Bob Gimlin know how to get the film site. They were both at the film site, but their memory has failed them. The excuse is that the men are older now; they simply have forgotten. Of course, Heironimus is older now as well. Therefore, the memory of where the film location was located is red herring.

But is there any evidence to prove Heironimus was the man in the suit?

Yes.

Heironimus said the Bigfoot suit smelled like dead horse hide.

I believe the suit was made from the hide of a dead bear. Either horse hide or bear hide, the suit smelled of old hide.

Heironimus said the head piece was like a football helmet with a leather mask.

Roger Patterson made a head piece that fit like a helmet. It was made of leather.

Heironimus said that Patterson and Gimlin helped Heironimus put on the suit and take off the suit.

With my copy of Patterson's suit, I needed help putting it on and taking it off.

Heironimus said that the longer he wore the suit and the head piece, the more nervous and claustrophobic he became.

In some tests on my suit, I wore it for hours, both the full suit and headpiece. I can say that I have experienced the same feelings and emotions as did Heironimus.

A key component of my film analysis was observations of how the PG Bigfoot walked. I noticed that when I focused on leg motion of the Bigfoot, I could see that there was a person inside the suit. Everyone knows that no two people walk the same. However, in the film the Bigfoot walks two different ways. In the first instance of walking in the beginning of the film, the Bigfoot's right foot extends outward and then straight up and down. Then, in the next leg-walk motion, the Bigfoot pushes off with its right foot.

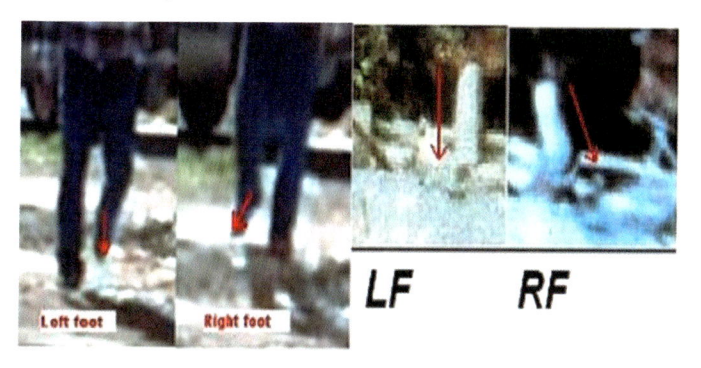

Close-up of the Bigfoot's feet and Bob Heironimus's feet.

The right foot pushes off and moves into an angle. As for the left foot, it stays in a straight up-and-down motion. Bob Heironimus walks this way as shown in the image.

When Heironimus walks, he pushes off with his right foot and when his right foot moves upward, the foot makes the same angle, pointing outward as does the foot in the Bigfoot. As Heironimus walks, his left foot makes an up-and-down motion just as does the Bigfoot.

The dynamics of Heironimus's and the Bigfoot's walking style are exactly the same. We can say for a fact that Heironimus was inside the Bigfoot suit in the PG Bigfoot film.

However, I believe two different men wore the same suit at two different times. Recall that Bob Heironimus took two polygraph test and passed them both. The first one he took was at the local police department in Yakima, his home town. The second polygraph test he took was administered on a late-1990s television show called *Lie Detector*.

The host of the show *Lie Detector* was Rolonda Watts.

On *Lie Detector*, Bob Heironimus took his second and last polygraph.

The polygraph administrators concluded that Bob Heironimus was the man in the Bigfoot suit in the 1967 Patterson Bigfoot film.

At the conclusion of *Lie Detector*, the host said that when the producers asked Patterson's attorney if they could buy rights to the P/G film for use in the program, they were told it would cost $10,000. Even then, if the film was to be used in a program featuring Bob Heironimus, the film would not be provided at any cost.

Due to this restriction, the producers bought the rights to use selected footage from two Bigfoot documentaries.

When the second part of the Bigfoot walking sequence is scrutinized, one sees the feet of the Bigfoot moving up and down in a synchronized motion. More, the Bigfoot walking in the second sequence is bigger than the Bigfoot in the first walking sequence.

Man walking in the tracking dog film.

While viewing the tracking dog film, I noticed one man in the film walking in the same manner as the Bigfoot walks in the second part of the Bigfoot film. As you see, the man on the far left of the film frame towers above all the other men seen in the film.

John Green is a tall man. He is about 6'2" to 6'4". The man on the far left in the film frame has to be well over 6'9".

249

This very tall man walks the same way as the Bigfoot walks in the second walking sequence in the P/G film. If the very tall man wore Patterson's Bigfoot suit, I estimate that the height of the Bigfoot would be about 7'2". The Bigfoot suit would add an extra five inches to the man's height. This is not an unreasonable height for the Bigfoot in the P/G film. I estimate that the Bigfoot is 7'4" tall in the second Bigfoot walking sequence.

The build on the very tall man is close to the same size and build of whoever wore the Bigfoot suit in the second Bigfoot walking sequence. No one knows this man's name. However, he was one of the men from Humboldt State who accompanied Jim McClarin to Bluff Creek.

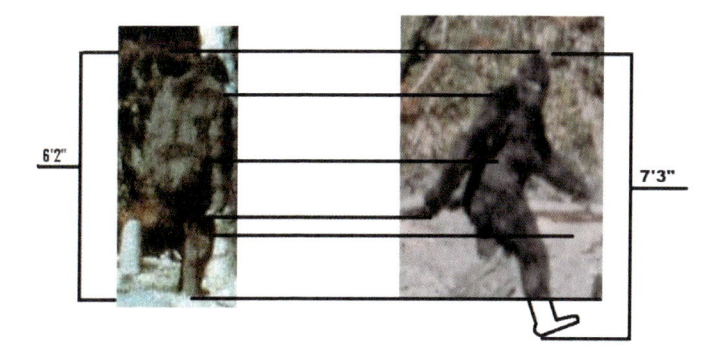

In the first Bigfoot walking sequence, Bob Heironimus wore the Bigfoot suit. In the second sequence, the very tall man did.

This explains why Bob Heironimus was never paid the $1,000 that Patterson promised to pay him for wearing the Bigfoot suit. The second sequence with the very tall man walking was issued as the original Patterson Bigfoot film, not the first sequence with Heironimus in the suit.

In 1968 when Ron Olson remade Patterson's documentary, the Heironimus walking sequence was edited into the remade documentary as the first walking sequence.

Chapter Thirteen: Walking Test

I decided to perform a test: Could I walk like the Bigfoot in the P/G film?

Usually producers try to find an athlete to walk like Patterson's Bigfoot for their own tests. The athlete always fails in performing the walk. The test is deemed a failure.

But, in the case of a hoax, it is better to find an ordinary person—a sort of man-off-the-street—and with a few instructions ask him to emulate the Bigfoot walk. In my case, I chose myself to perform the walk.

Shown above are still frames from a video my test partner (Tim Beckholt) shot of myself attempting to walk the same as the Bigfoot in the film. I only had to run the test one time since in one try I successfully walked like the Bigfoot in the P/G film. This test proves that an ordinary person can walk like the Bigfoot.

In another test, I produced Bigfoot tracks and Bigfoot casts.

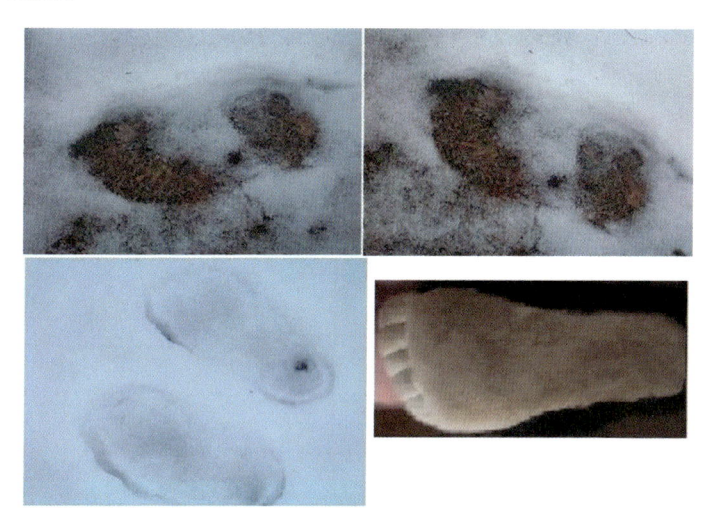

The image above shows the test Bigfoot shoe I made to go along with the Bigfoot suit. I used the shoe to make a fake Bigfoot track in snow. In the image, one can see a break in the middle section of the foot. Some researchers state emphatically that no one can make a fake Bigfoot print in the ground that shows a break in the middle of the foot. However, I show such a break in my test Bigfoot track.

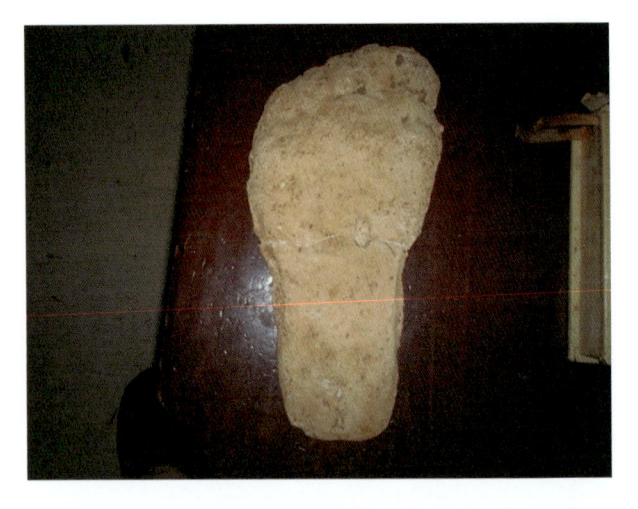

Above is an image of one of the cast prints I made. I made the cast print from one of the Bigfoot shoes that I made.

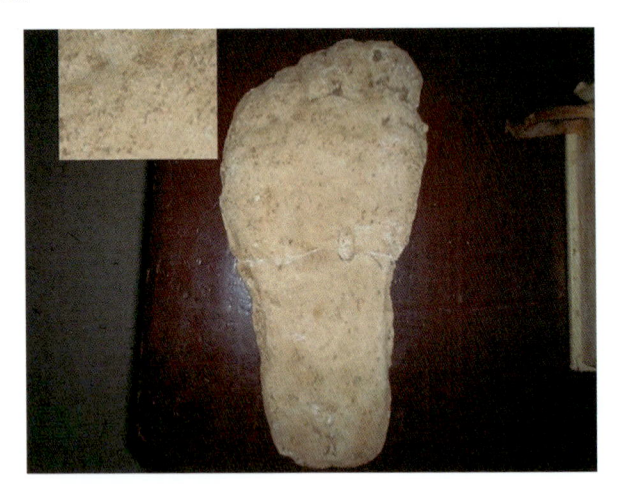

Dermal ridging can be seen in the cast print. Again, some researchers state that a human being cannot create

254

such dermal ridging in a fake Bigfoot shoe. However, once again I proved the critics wrong.

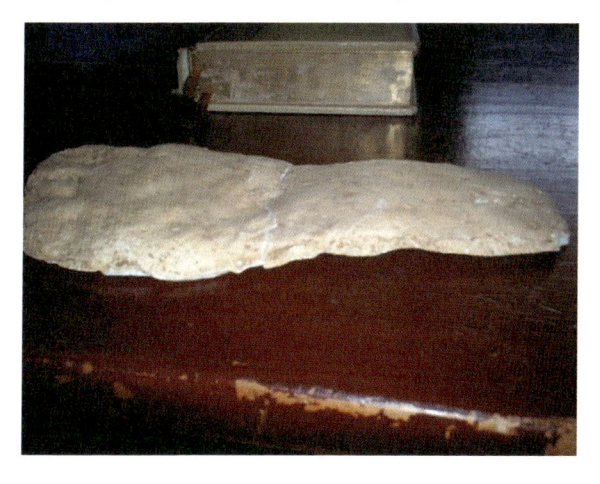

In another image, the side view of the cast print is shown. The mid-break in the middle of the foot is visible. And in this image of the cast print has dermal ridging and a break in the middle of the foot.

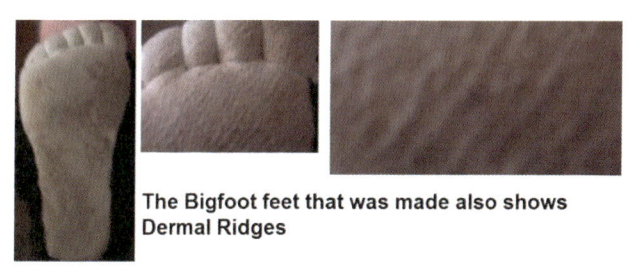

The Bigfoot feet that was made also shows Dermal Ridges

Dermal ridges can be seen on the bottom of the fake Bigfoot shoes shown in the image above.

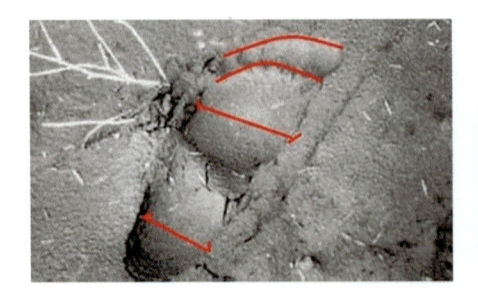

No match. Two different tracks

The image above is of a cast print Patterson said he made. He claimed the cast print was taken from one of the foot prints left by the Bigfoot in his film. However, also shown is a photo taken of one of the Bigfoot tracks found in the Bluff Creek area one day after Patterson filmed the Bigfoot.

These two prints are different in type and size. They clearly are not the same.

Let's pay special attention to the Bigfoot track in the photo below. Is it truly real?

The photo of the Bigfoot track from the P/G Bigfoot film site is usually reproduced in various articles in close-up format. However, I managed to secure a copy of the full-size image. The full-sized image is reproduced here.

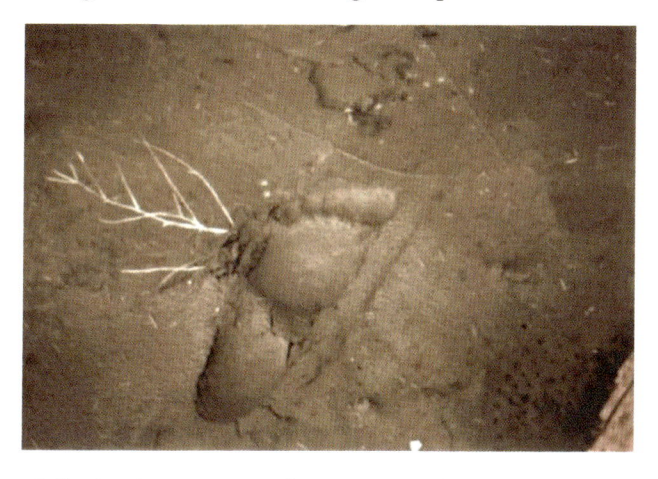

The full size image reveals more detail.

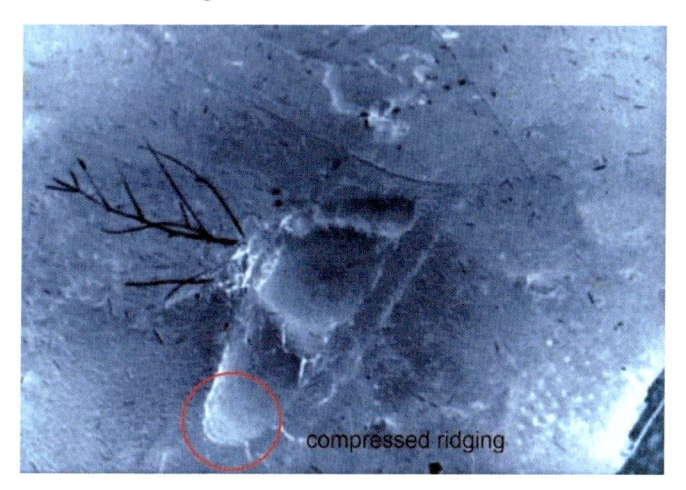

257

Tire track

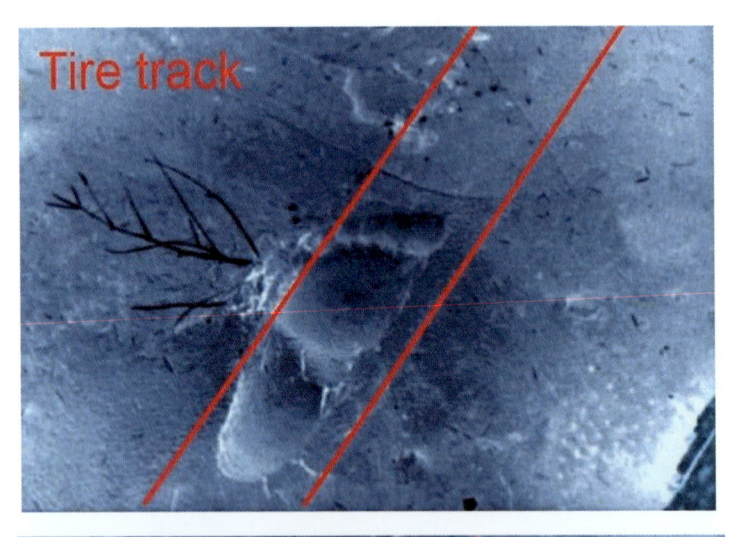

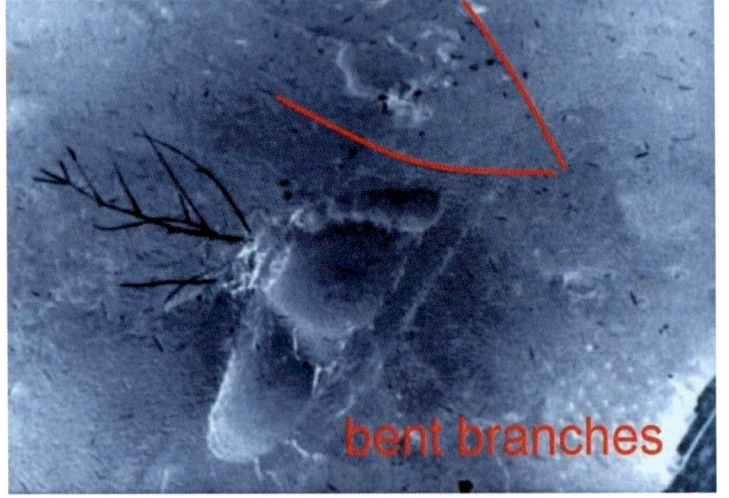

bent branches

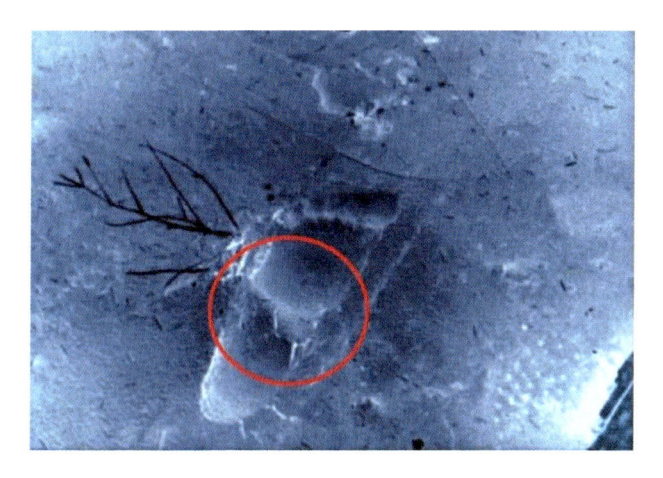

The full-size image is of a fake Bigfoot track. The image shows the detail of a tire that was rolled over the track; the outline of the tire's track can be seen. We also see bent branches across the track, ridging on the back of the feel, and a break in the middle of the foot.

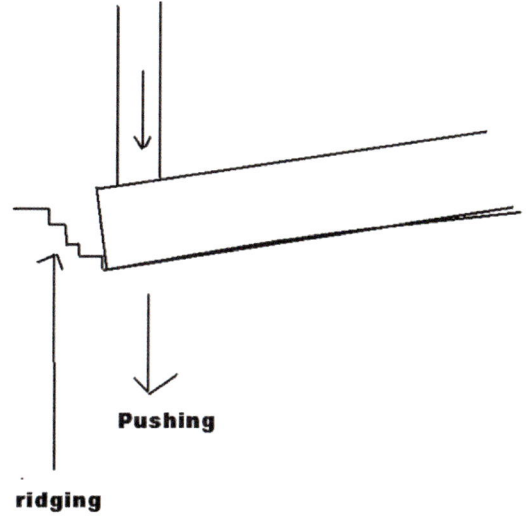

Pushing

ridging

259

Compressed ridges

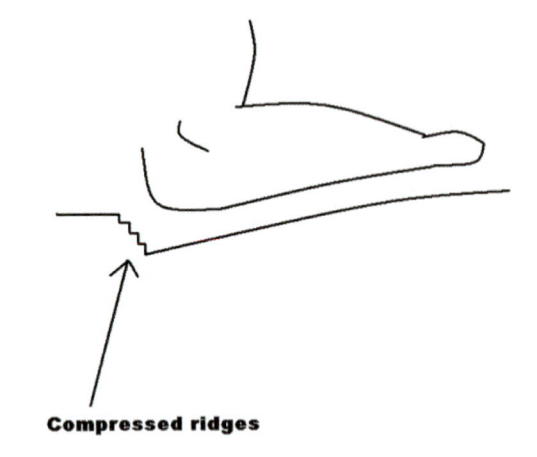

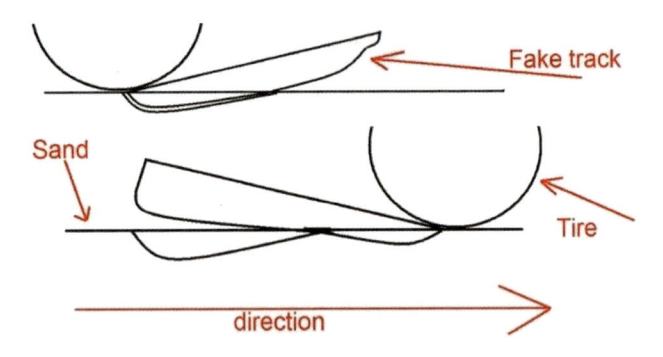

Fake track

Sand

Tire

direction

In the accompanying diagram, I show how the Bigfoot track was made. First, let's look at the Bigfoot track from the film site.

Test 1

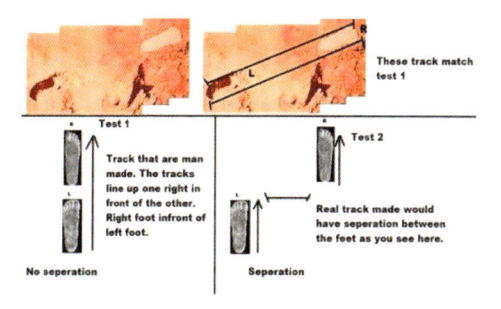

Track that are man made. The tracks line up one right in front of the other. Right foot infront of left foot.

No seperation

Test 2

These track match test 1

Real track made would have seperation between the feet as you see here.

Seperation

It has been claimed that the distance of the Bigfoot track from another one was about 60 inches, and that no walking man can make tracks using fake Bigfoot feet (shoes) that far apart.

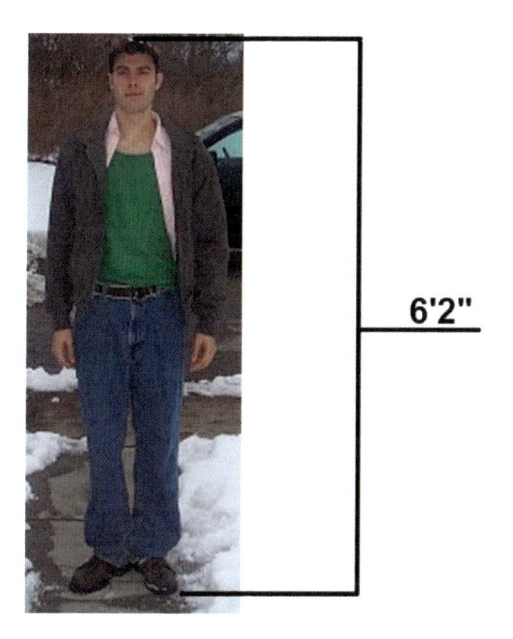

6'2"

The image above is of my nephew Tim Beckholt. He worked with me over several years performing tests on

261

the P/G film. In the particular test described here, he wore the Bigfoot shoes I made. I instructed him to run with the fake Bigfoot shoes on his feet.

A frame from a video of Tim Beckholt running in Bigfoot shoes.

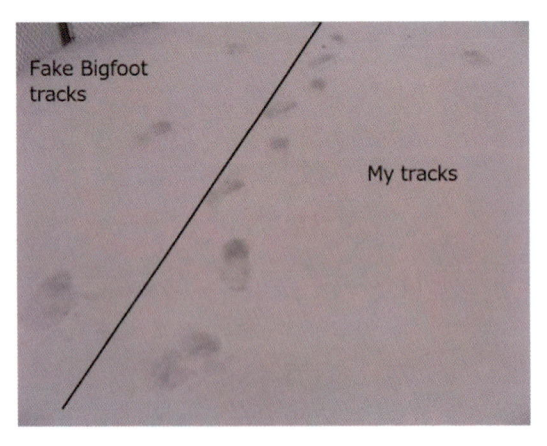

In the left of this frame, we see the fake Bigfoot tracks Tim Beckholt impressed into the ground as he ran. On the right are my prints with normal footwear and just a normal walk for a man.

The distance between the front of the toes of the right foot to the back of the heel of the left foot of one set of Tim Beckholt's tracks measured 64 inches.

The test was done on level ground. However, in the second test, Bigfoot tracks were made on a hillside.

When we measured the distance between the toes of the right foot to the heel of the left foot in the track series impressed into the hillside, we arrived at 68 inches.

I then preform other test to compere to.

In all my years of researching Bigfoot, I found little evidence of real Bigfoot tracks. More than 80% of the Bigfoot tracks I have seen are fakes.

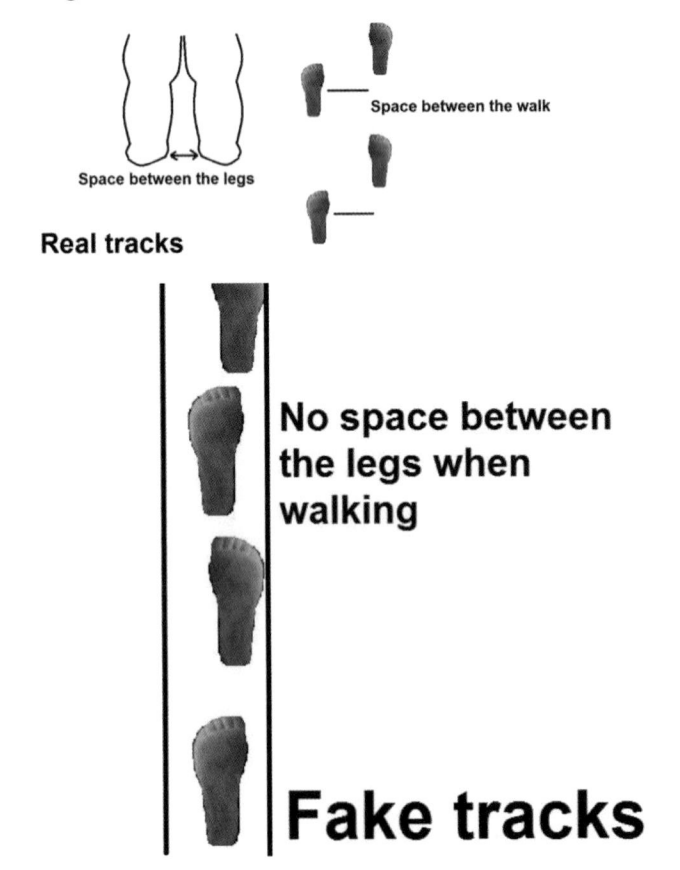

Space between the legs

Space between the walk

Real tracks

No space between the legs when walking

Fake tracks

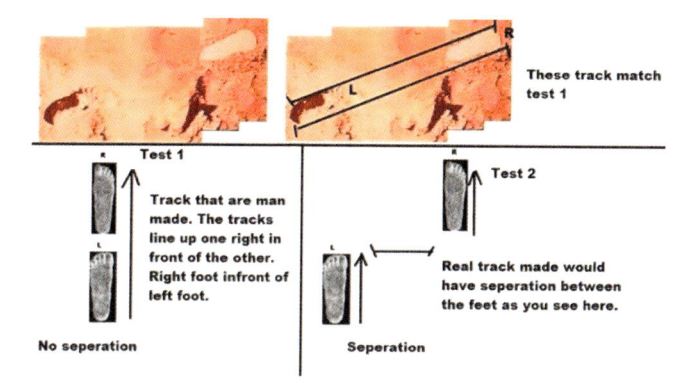

Test 1 — Track that are man made. The tracks line up one right in front of the other. Right foot infront of left foot. **No seperation**

Test 2 — Real track made would have separation between the feet as you see here. **Seperation**

These track match test 1

The Bigfoot tracks in the Patterson film and John Green film were manmade.

By looking over the tracks and doing test I found no space or separations between the tracks. Rather, the tracks were arranged in the ground in a straight line as would be the case when someone walks with fake Bigfoot tracks strapped to his feet.

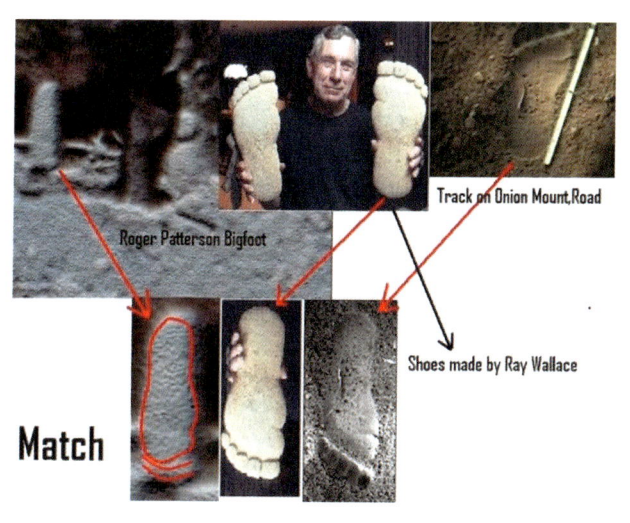

Roger Patterson Bigfoot

Track on Onion Mount, Road

Shoes made by Ray Wallace

Match

265

The feet on Roger Patterson's Bigfoot match the same Bigfoot shoes made by Ray Wallace. (Ray Wallace was the owner of a construction company working on the Bluff Creek logging road project. He admitted to his family that he had a long history of making fake Bigfoot tracks, and films.) The Bigfoot tracks seen in the tracking dog film also match Ray Wallace's Bigfoot shoes.

The Bigfoot tracks that Roger Patterson filmed and the Bigfoot tracks seen in the tracking dog film were made by the same person.

So you see by these test we have done and by finding this information from these test, we can now tell a real Bigfoot track from a fake Bigfoot track.

For if the track was real we should see separations between the legs by the impression of the tracks. And we should see more detail on how the creature made in the impression of the track. But if we see tracks made by the testing I have and shown then they are manmade tracks/fake Bigfoot tracks.

Chapter Fourteen: Who filmed Roger Patterson?

For years, people thought that Roger Patterson or Bob Gimlin shot the P/G film. However, interviews with Bob Gimlin open up new questions as to who really filmed the PG Bigfoot. Gimlin has always claimed he never used Patterson's camera, and that Roger always kept the camera on his own person.

My research, photographic evidence from the film, other images, and review of Gimlin interviews demonstrate that the only person seen in Patterson's first documentary is Roger Patterson.

Therefore, who was always filming Patterson? If not Bob Gimlin, who was it?

I have determined that one and the same camera was always used in filming. The filming includes the P/G film, the tracking dog film, and the Jim McClarin walking-the-path-of-the-Bigfoot film. I have concluded that it was John Green's camera that filmed all three films. We will go over the camera as we go along.

But who was behind the camera?

First, we consider Roger Patterson. Patterson is always riding a horse in his documentary. The only time we do not see Patterson is during the Bluff Creek Bigfoot walking film; all we see is the Bigfoot.

Bob Gimlin did not film any of the P/G film because he said that Patterson had the camera with him the whole time and that he, Gimlin, never used a camera or knew how to work a camera. The only time Bob Gimlin is seen in the Bigfoot film is, as I have shown, in the first Bigfoot walking sequence (he is standing behind brush).

To understand who used the camera in all three films, consider the following diagram.

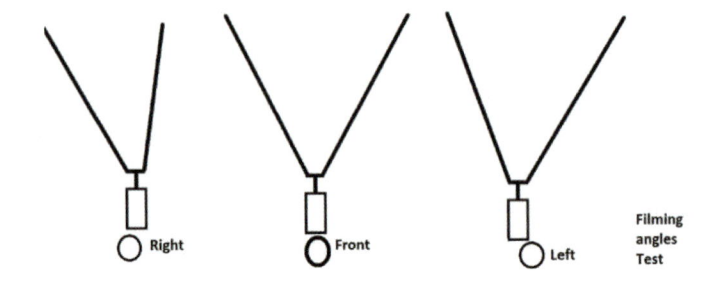

Right   Front   Left   Filming angles Test

The diagram shows us the angle at which the film was shot; and if the camera man was filming from the front of his body, or from his left or his right.

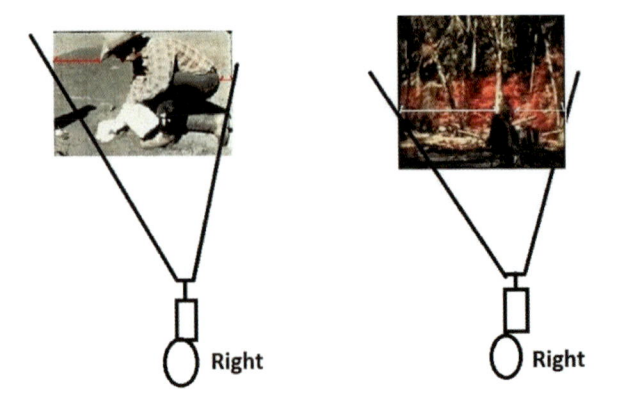

Right   Right

268

The film itself shows that the camera man was filming from his right.

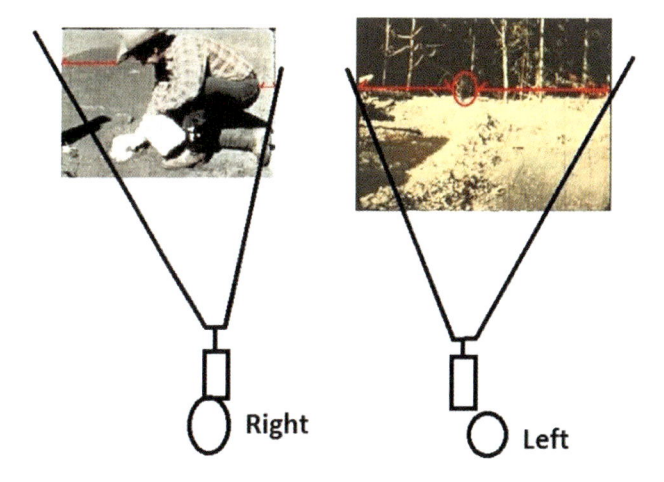

However, when we concentrate on the Bigfoot film at its start, we see that the camera man was filming from his left. Most of the P/G film was shot by a right handed person but only the part of the Bigfoot walking was filmed by a left handed person.

269

When viewing the tracking dog film, we see that the camera man was filming from his right.

We can also see that when the camera man was filming, he first films the subject or person in front of the camera; then the camera man pans off to the left or off to the right to show the forest surroundings.

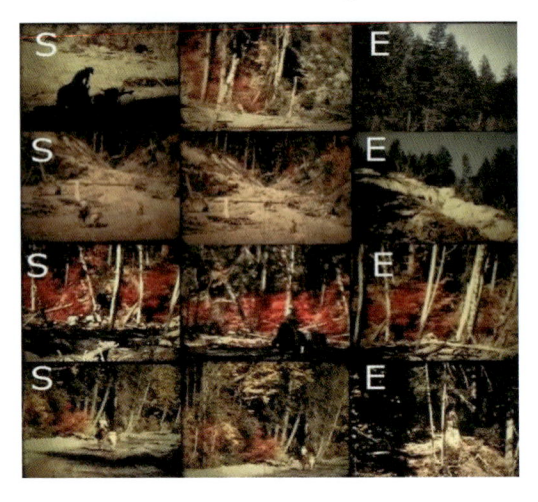

Likewise, in the P/G film we can see the camera man filming the subject or person in front of the camera. Then, he pans to the left or right as he films the forest surroundings.

By this analysis, we conclude that the same man filmed the tracking dog film, the P/G film, and Roger Patterson. As it was reported and based on images shot in the Blue Creek Mountain area, Rene Dahinden filmed the tracking dog film. And by this new evidence he also shot most of the P/G Bigfoot film.

What type of camera was used to shoot the films?

As it has been reported, Patterson used a rental camera, a 16-mm Kodak K-100 model.

That camera has long been declared the camera that Roger Patterson used to film his Bigfoot… or was it?

In my research, I discovered that the Bigfoot film was edited twice. Sound was also added to the film. The film was printed on 16-mm Kodachrome film. But was this the camera used to shoot Patterson and Gimlin's Bigfoot film?

Few people know it, but Patterson himself never said what type of camera he used. The Kodak K-100 model claimed to be the camera he used came into play when Patterson did not return a camera to a rental store in Yakima. He rented a camera from Sheppard's Camera Store. The county sheriff sent out an arrest warrant to have Patterson arrested. There is no evidence to show that the camera was a K-100.

However, by studying the film itself, we can find out what type of camera Roger used.

First, remember that Patterson did a lot of filming at the end of 1966, and he did a lot of filming in 1967. This we know from looking at a number of film frames shown earlier in this book.

Roger only rented the camera from Sheppard's for about three months. However, he was, in fact, filming for a whole year. Therefore, who was with Patterson when he was repeatedly filmed riding on horses, pouring the bigfoot cast, and other scenes?

Remember that in 1967, Patterson was on a Bigfoot expedition. This can be proven by some of the films that was shot. These films show Roger with John Green and Rene Dahendin.

In the tracking dog film, a camera was used to film the Bigfoot tracks and all the men that was with them.

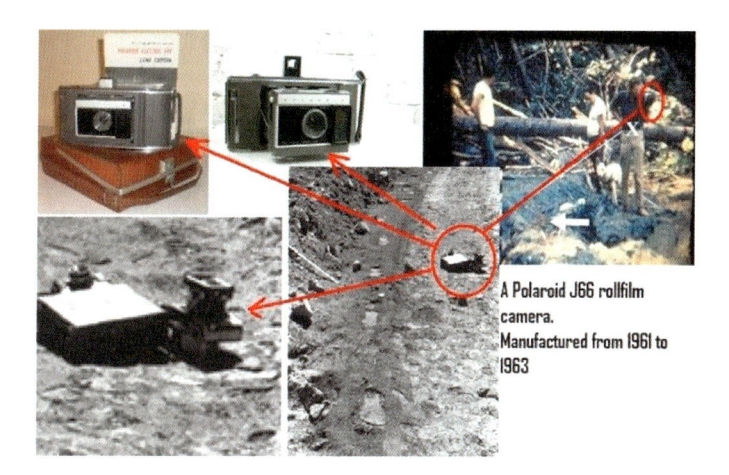

A Polaroid J66 rollfilm camera. Manufactured from 1961 to 1963

John Green had two cameras with him as the tracking dog film was shot. The first camera was a still camera, a Polaroid J66. The second camera was a Keystone K-50, a 16-mm camera.

Green and Dahinden used the Keystone K-50 when they filmed the tracking dog film and the film of Jim McClarin walking the path of the Bigfoot.

But when did Patterson use Green's camera?

When analyzing all three films (P/G film, Tracking dog film, Jim McClarin film), I found markings on every third frame in each film.

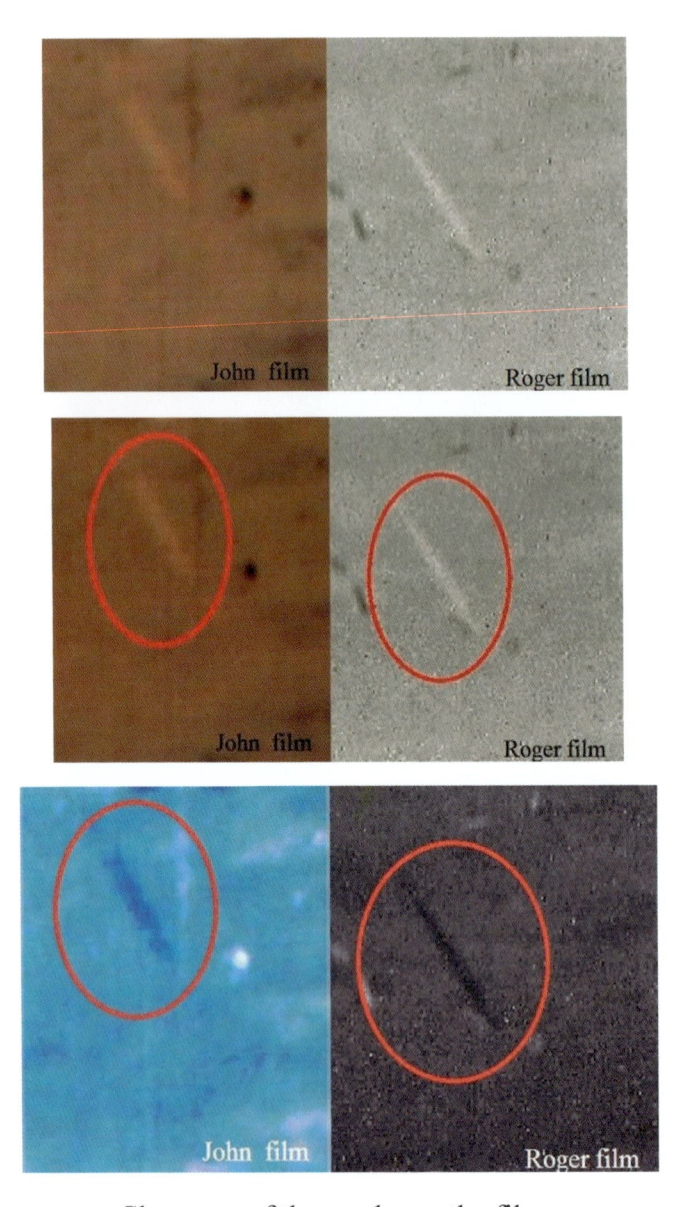

Close-ups of the marks on the films.

The frame on the left is a close up from the McClarin film. The frame on the right is from the P/G film.

In every third frame in the films, the mark shows up on the bottom left corner of every third frame in these films.

The same marking on all three films indicates that the three films were shot using the same camera.

With this new evidence, we know that Patterson filmed the Bigfoot using John Green's camera, the Keystone K-50.

Chapter Fifteen: Notes

1) In December of 2011, the pilot Keith Chiazzari read about a "massacre" in Bluff Creek. After reading it the article he claimed there was no massacre. He confirmed that he flew John Green and Rene Dahinden down to Bluff Creek, and although Green and Dahinden did have a gun, it was never used.
2) In Grover Krantz's book *Big Footprints*, Krantz discussed how a person can make Bigfoot prints with his fingers or hand tools. In his discussion, Krantz states that Roger Patterson told him that he did the same thing in his documentary and made plaster casts of them! Amazingly, a few days later he filmed an actual Sasquatch.

This statement proves that Roger made fake Bigfoot tracks. Since Bob Gimlin was with Roger when he filmed the Bigfoot, he knew that Roger was making fake Bigfoot tracks and plaster casts of fake Bigfoot tracks.

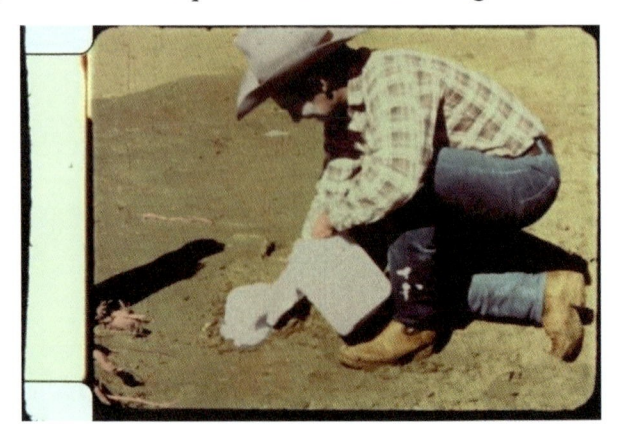

Was this the fake Bigfoot track Roger Patterson made, as told to Krantz?

When viewing the print up close, it does in fact look like a manmade track. The sides of the print should be level with the ground. Instead, the sides look as if the print was shaped in the soil using a tool.

3) Jim McClarin was interviewed by Al Tostado of the *Times-Standard* in 1967.

McClarin is asked when he started working on his Bigfoot statue in Willow Creek. McClarin replies he does not know the actual start date. However, it was most likely in the summer time when Patterson filmed his Bigfoot in Bluff Creek.

As the story goes, Patterson and Gimlin claimed they filmed the Bigfoot in October of 1967. But in an interview, McClarin stated that Patterson told him that the film was shot in the summer time. Summer ends on Labor Day weekend. Therefore, the film was shot in the summer, not in October of 1967.

4) In an interview, Ivan T. Sanderson reported that one night in 1967 Jim McClarin contacted him by phone and told him about Roger Patterson filming the Bigfoot and that Roger was on his way to get the film processed.

5) According to Grover Krantz, years later after Roger Patterson and Bob Gimlin filmed the Bigfoot, they said that they should have shot the creature for more financial gain to shut up the non-believers.

6) According to Jerry Merritt, he said that he and Patterson should have tried to get more backers to further fund Patterson's Bigfoot movie, but they had no luck in doing so. Then when Roger Patterson died, Ron Olson of ANE took over Roger's documentary, remade it, and renamed it to *Sasquatch - The Legend of Bigfoot*. Patterson received no credit.

Roger Patterson's documentary and Ron Olson's documentary are very much the same. In an interview, Jerry Merritt's statements support my findings that Roger's documentary was remade by Ron Olson.

Merritt traveled with Patterson driving back and forth to Hollywood visiting friends and entertainers. They talked to Gene Vincent and Ross Hagen. Ross Hagen starred in a TV show called *Daktari*. He helped Patterson write and record a song in Hollywood for Roger's documentary.

Final Thoughts

In my 11 years of research/investigation into the P/G Bluff Creek Bigfoot film, I never set out to put anyone down or expose anyone as a hoaxer.

The aim of my research was to look for the truth through evidence. The evidence convinced me that the PG film is, indeed, a hoax.

However, should we look at this one film as a hoax?

I think not.

I say this because the Patterson-Gimlin story transcends this single film. Lasting 50 years, the PG film makes for a great story, impacting countless people's imagination all over the world and motivating many to track down and capture this mysterious over-sized, hairy monolith.

A handful of men were looking for Bigfoot in 1967. Today, thousands of people are on the adventure of their lives to finally reveal the real truth of Bigfoot to the world.

For you, is the film a hoax or a film that serves as a starting point for a new adventure?

You be the judge!

God Bless.

Leroy Blevins Sr.

Here is some of the images from my research on the Patterson and Gimlin Bigfoot film I have restored and colorized. The reason for me to restore the images and colorized them was to get more details out of each image or film frame. I do this proses in all of the research I have done even in my research on the JFK Assassination.

Enjoy.

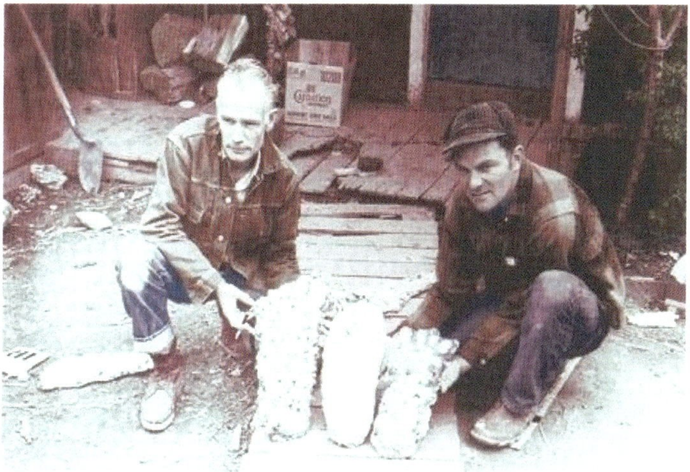

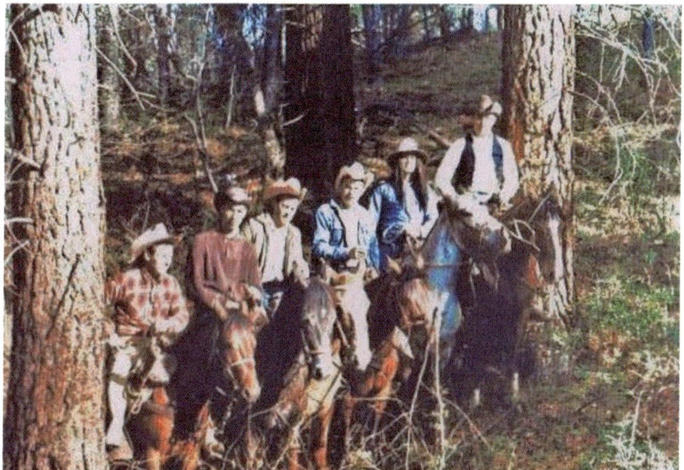

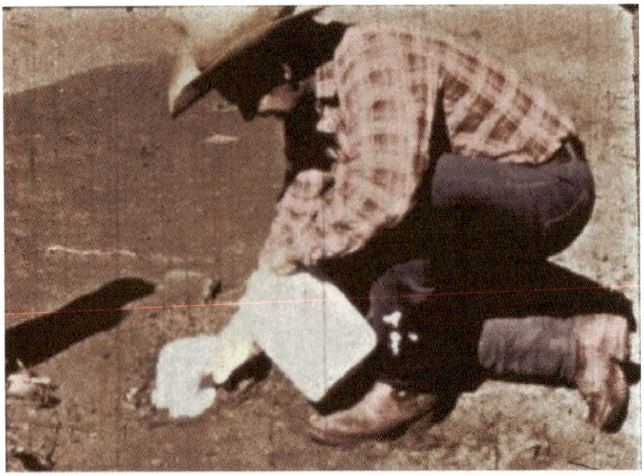

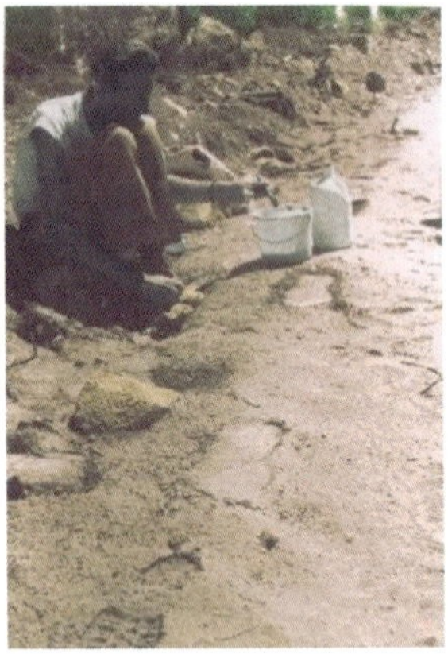

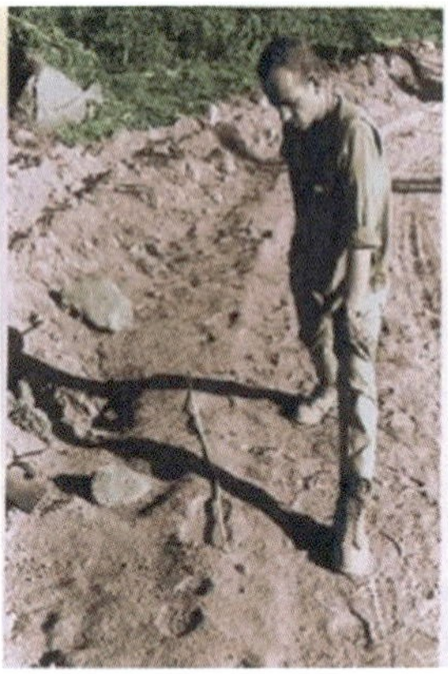

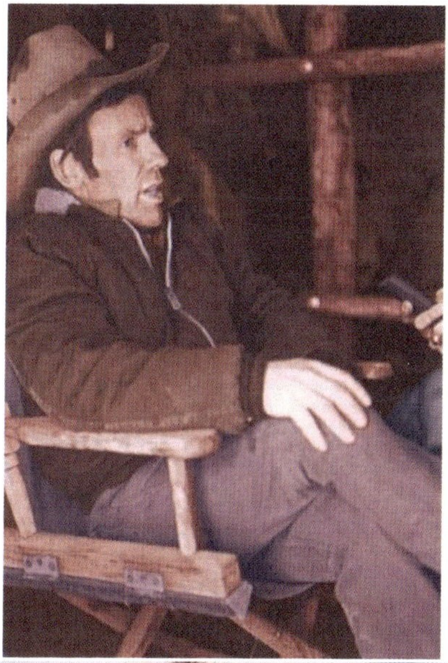

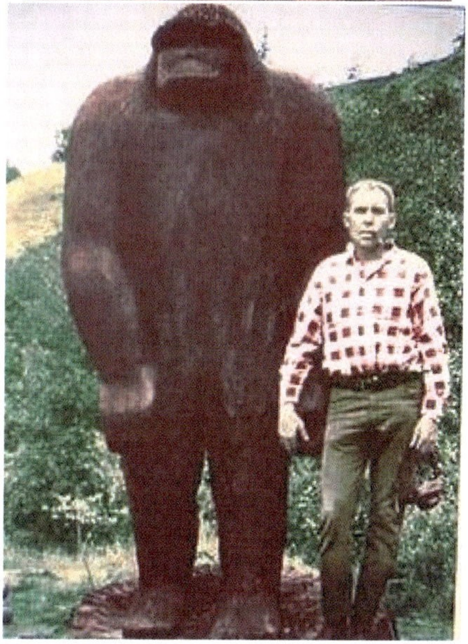

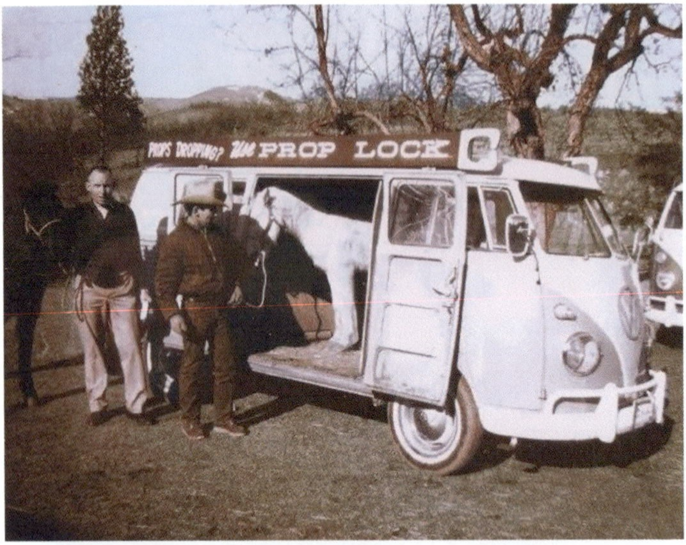
PROPS DROPPING? Use PROP LOCK

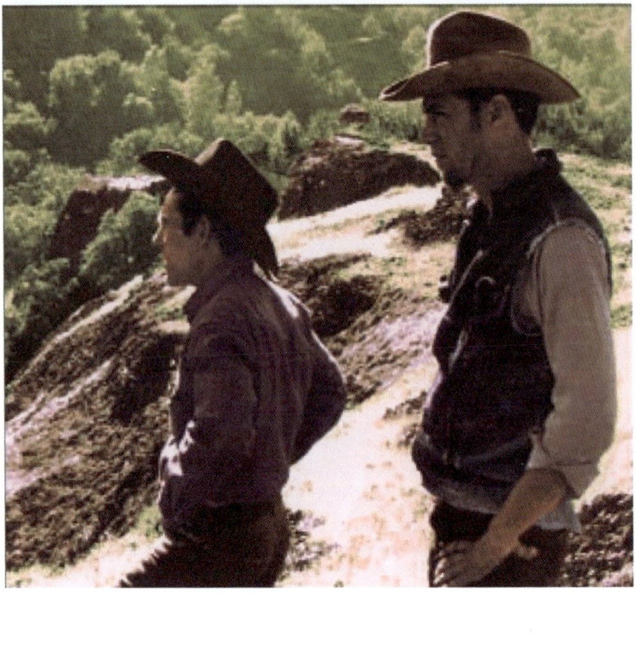

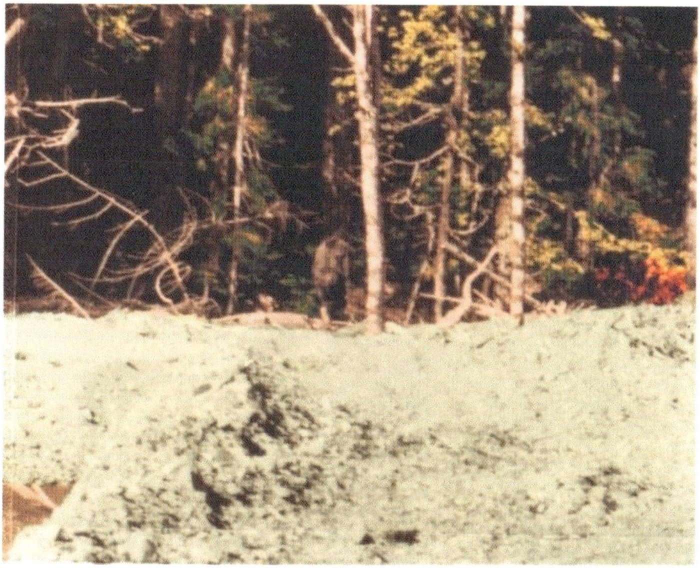

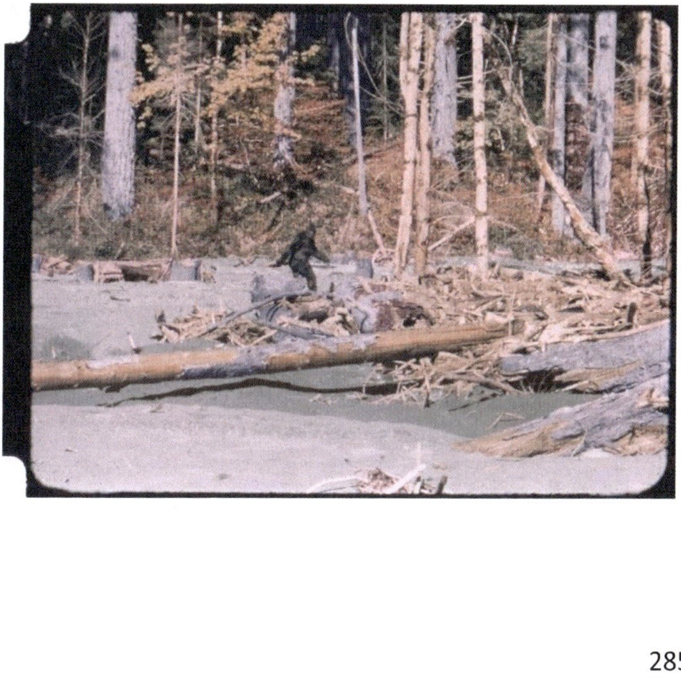

Other available research books:

Evidence of a conspiracy: JFK Assassination

JFK Assassination Colorized Images

Evidence Files: Case Closed

Who Murdered JFK?

Noah's Ark

Printed in Poland
by Amazon Fulfillment
Poland Sp. z o.o., Wrocław